Grammar Games and Activities for Teachers

Peter Watcyn-Jones
Illustrated by Bruce Hogarth

To Polly, Philippa and other teachers I have met
whose kind comments make me want to go on writing books

PENGUIN BOOKS

PENGUIN BOOKS

Published by the Penguin Group
Penguin Books Ltd, 27 Wrights Lane, London W8 5TZ, England
Penguin Books USA Inc., 375 Hudson Street, New York, New York 10014, USA
Penguin Books Australia Ltd, Ringwood, Victoria, Australia
Penguin Books Canada Ltd, 10 Alcorn Avenue, Toronto, Ontario, Canada M4V 3B2
Penguin Books (NZ) Ltd, 182–190 Wairau Road, Auckland 10, New Zealand

Penguin Books Ltd, Registered Offices: Harmondsworth, Middlesex, England

Published by Penguin Books 1995
10 9 8 7 6 5 4 3 2

The moral right of the author and illustrator has been asserted

Every effort has been made to trace copyright holders in every case. The publishers would
be interested to hear from any not acknowledged here

Printed in England by William Clowes Limited, Beccles and London
Set in New Century Schoolbook

The publishers make grateful acknowledgement to the following for permission to reprint
copyright photographs:
p. 63: Adrian C. Muttitt/Barnaby's Picture Library (top left), Studio Seven Photography/
Barnaby's Picture Library (top right), Day Williams/Barnaby's Picture Library (bottom
left), Day Williams/Barnaby's Picture Library (bottom right); p. 64: Anne Crabbe/
Barnaby's Picture Library (left), David Simpson/Barnaby's Picture Library (right);
p. 166: Sylvia Collins/Barnaby's Picture Library; p.167: Graham Alcock/Barnaby's
Picture Library (top left), B. Gibbs/Barnaby's Picture Library (top right), /Barnaby's
Picture Library (centre left), Lucette Aldis/Barnaby's Picture Library (centre right),
Nick Scott/Barnaby's Picture Library (bottom)

Contents

Contents

Introduction

Grammar Games and Activities is the second book in a series of source book for teachers. It contains a collection of 120 activities for practising and revising grammar. They range from elementary to advanced activities, all of which contain material to be photocopied. It is hoped they will prove useful in general courses to give extra practice in grammar.

The choice of which grammatical items to include in the book is largely subjective, with the emphasis on those most frequently encountered – in particular asking and answering questions in various tenses. There are bound to be omissions, but it is hoped that there are enough basic ideas in this book to encourage and stimulate teachers to devise their own activities for any grammatical items that have been left out.

Most of the activities in this book involve the students working in pairs or groups. Apart from making the learning process more dynamic and enjoyable it may also help make a traditionally serious subject like grammar more "user friendly".

The majority of the ideas in this book are based on ideas I first used while teaching in Scandinavia. There is always, however, the problem of knowing who came up with a particular idea first. Where I have consciously used someone else's idea I have of course acknowledged this. In other cases where I have devised an activity which someone else feels he or she can lay prior claim to then I apologize and will gladly make the appropriate acknowledgement in future editions of this book.

The organisation of this book

The activities have not been grouped according to grammatical structures. Instead I decided to group them according to types of activities. Altogether there are eleven sections: *Find someone activities, Bingo activities, Jigsaw reading activities, Asking and answering questions activities, Information-gap activities, Find the differences activities, Questionnaires and surveys, Giving and receiving instructions activities, Board and card games, etc., Teacher-led activities,* and *Miscellaneous activities.* Part 1 of the book gives detailed teacher's notes for each activity while Part 2 contains the various cards, handouts, etc. to be photocopied.

Where possible, the material to be photocopied has been arranged in such a way that it also serves as an instant key to the majority of the activities. For example, in the jigsaw reading activities the broken sentences are arranged on the page in the correct order. It is therefore important to remember to shuffle the cards prior to handing them out to the students. Where a key is not obvious from the layout, a separate key is included in the teacher's notes.

Classroom organisation

Although class sizes vary considerably, the book assumes an average class size of 10–20 students. Where possible, the classroom should be physically rearranged to facilitate working in pairs or groups. However, should this not be possible, even the more traditional front-facing rows of desks can be easily adapted for pair work and group work. For pair work, students can either work with the person sitting next to them or the person in front of or behind them. For group work, two students can easily turn their chairs round to face two others behind them. Where you have an uneven number of students in the class, most pair work activities can be done by three people (if necessary, two students against one).

The role of the teacher

Apart from the activities in the section *Teacher-led activities*, the teacher's role is largely that of coordinator. He or she is mainly responsible for:

- preparing the material in sufficient quantities
- explaining clearly what is to be done
- "checking" answers at the end of an activity

Once an activity has started, students usually work independently of the teacher at their own pace. The teacher goes round the classroom listening and monitoring their progress and only interfering or helping if *absolutely necessary*.

Time limits

Although many teachers may disagree with me on this point, I strongly advise giving the class a time limit for most of the activities, and to stop them whether they have finished or not. Apart from the obvious difficulties of students finishing at different times, the checking process is often an integral and, from the learning point of view, important part of the activity. As such it is better that you check with the whole class rather than individual groups.

Storing the material

The material to be photocopied can be divided into two types: (a) handouts which the students write on, and (b) material which the students use but do not write on.

To save the teacher unnecessary work, therefore, it is a good idea that material that can be re-used is made as durable as possible. One way is to mount everything on thin card. (Many photocopiers nowadays allow the use of card.) These cards and handouts can then be stored in separate envelopes (clearly labelled on the outside) which can be handed back to the teacher at the end of the activity.

All of the activities presented in this book require preparation on the part of the teacher. It is hoped that all the extra effort will prove to be rewarding.

Part 1 Teacher's notes

Find someone activities

1 Find someone who...1
Intermediate/Advanced

This activity has been around for some time, but is still very useful for practising forming, asking and answering questions.

Grammar points

Asking questions (various tenses); Short Yes/No answers

Method

1 Copy and cut up the cards on pages 29–30, so there is one for each student in the class.

2 Give out the cards and allow time for the students to work out which questions to ask.

3 Students now walk around the room trying to find answers to the five questions on their cards. To ensure that they talk to as many people as possible, tell them that they are only allowed to ask *one question* every time they talk to someone.

4 Students write down any answers to their questions, plus the name of the student who gave them the answer.

5 After a while, stop the activity, irrespective of whether everyone has found answers to all their questions.

6 As a quick follow-up, let each student read out one of the answers on his/her card. You might also take up any questions for which the students couldn't get answers.

2 Find someone who...2
Elementary

This is a variation of the above activity where, instead of the students getting individual cards, they all have a copy of the same handout.

Grammar points

Asking questions (Present Simple); Short Yes/No answers; longer answers to WH- questions

Method

1 Give each student a copy of the handout on page 31.

2 As Activity 1, though students can now be allowed to

ask two to three questions every time they talk to someone. If they get a Yes-answer, they follow it up by asking for further details.

3 This time, as a follow-up, you could go through all the questions, each student answering a different one.

3 Find someone who...3
Intermediate/Advanced

Grammar points

Asking questions (Perfect Simple/Past Simple); Short Yes/ No answers; longer answers to WH- questions

Method

As Activity 2. The handout is on page 32.

4 Is it true or false?
Intermediate

In this activity students have to find out whether certain statements about their group are true or false.

Grammar points

Asking questions (various tenses); Short Yes/No answers

Method

1 Divide the class into groups of up to 10 students. Give each student a copy of the handout on page 33. Allow them time to work out what sort of questions to ask to check whether the ten statements are true or false, e.g., *Have you ever visited Rome? Were you born in June?* or *When were you born?* etc.

2 Students now work as a group trying to find out whether the ten statements are true or not. To help them, ten boxes are included at the bottom of the page to write the names of any students who answer Yes to any question.

3 At the end of the activity, the group make a note on their handout of which statements are true or false.

4 Check orally with each group. You don't have to go through all ten statements. You can instead ask one group for any facts that were true and another for any facts that were false, and so on.

5 Find out likes and dislikes
Intermediate

This is another variation, this time for groups of eight students.

1

Grammar points

Asking questions (Do you like…?); Short Yes/No answers

Method

1 Divide the class into groups of 8 students. Copy and cut out the cards on page 34 and give one to each student. Explain that each person likes one thing and dislikes something else. But they also have to find out about other people's likes and dislikes.

2 Students now work in their group, taking it in turn to ask and answer questions in an effort to find who likes and dislikes the two items on their cards.

3 Check orally. Each student can tell you one thing they found out.

---

6 Trivia search   *Intermediate/Advanced*

This is a slightly more difficult version of Activity 5. This time, each person knows three items of trivia and has to find the answers to three others. This activity is for groups of six students.

Grammar points

Asking WH- questions (various tenses); Short Yes/No answers

Method

As activity 5. The handout is on page 35.

---

7 Group opinions   *Intermediate*

This time students will use tag questions to find answers to their questions.

Grammar points

Tag questions (various); Short Yes/No answers; All of us, most of us, none of us, etc.

Method

1 Divide the class into groups of 5–8 students. Each student gets a copy of the handout on page 36. Explain that each person has to interview every member of the group to find out, for example, how many of the group don't trust politicians, prefer tea to coffee, etc. But this time, instead of asking a direct question, they have to ask a tag question each time, e.g. *You don't trust politicians, do you?* or *You trust politicians, don't you?* They record their answers by putting a cross (X) in the boxes numbered 1–8.

2 Students now interview each other and make a note of the answers on their handouts.

3 When they have finished, they add up the crosses next to each statement and from this work out how many of the group do the various things using the words at the bottom of the page, *All of us…, Most of us…, Hardly any of us…, etc..*

4 Check orally. One or two students from each group can tell you one or two things they found out.

Bingo activities

Although teachers may tire of bingo, students rarely do, and for sheer concentration there are few activities that can beat it. The activities described here are variations of bingo. For each activity there are ten different bingo cards. For larger classes, some students can work in pairs.

---

8 What's the time bingo   *Elementary*

In this game the students have drawings of clocks showing various times

Grammar points

Telling the time (It's one o'clock, etc.)

Method

1 Copy and cut out the ten bingo cards on page 40. Also make two copies of the teacher's board on page 37. Leave one copy as it is but cut the other copy into 20 squares.

2 Give the students a card each. Allow a few minutes for them to look through them before beginning.

3 Put the 20 squares in a hat, cup, etc. Draw them out one at a time. You can either say the time, e.g. *It's five past two, It's half past eight,* etc., or you can do it as a student-teacher dialogue, where different students ask you *What's the time?* when you draw a card. You answer, *It's twenty to seven, etc.* before placing the square on your "master board". If the students have a clock on their card showing that time, they cross it out.

4 Play proceeds until a student has crossed out every picture, in which case (s)he shouts *Bingo!*

5 Check by getting him/her to tell you the time on each picture (s)he has crossed out. (You can ask another student to monitor this, to avoid any cheating!)

---

9 Irregular verbs bingo
Elementary/Intermediate

In this game, the students have the infinitive of various irregular verbs. The teacher's board contains the three forms of each verb (*infinitive, past, past participle*).

Grammar points

Irregular verbs (3 forms)

Method

As Activity 8. The teacher explains that (s)he is going to call out the past tense of each verb. To check, the winning student can read out all three parts of each verb. The student cards are on page 41 and the teacher's board is on page 37.

10 Telephone number bingo   *Elementary*

In this game, the students have to listen to various telephone numbers being read out.

Grammar points

Numbers (as used in telephone numbers)

Method

As Activity 8. As in Activity 8 this could be done as a student-teacher dialogue, namely:

Student: *What's your telephone number?*
Teacher: *(taking card from hat) It's 3–4–double 5–7–8. etc.*

The student cards are on page 42 and the teacher's board is on page 38.

11 Prepositions bingo   *Intermediate*

The bingo cards here are slightly different from normal: each one consists of five sentences with missing prepositions. As each preposition is called out the students write them in the gaps on their cards. At the end of the game the winning student reads out all five sentences.

Grammar points

Prepositions (general)

Method

As Activity 8, though it is a good idea to let the students read through the sentences first to work out which prepositions to listen for. The student cards are on page 43 and the teacher's board is on page 38.

12 Conjunctions bingo
Intermediate/Advanced

This is similar to Activity 11, but this time a conjunction rather than a preposition is missing from each sentence.

Grammar points

Conjunctions (although, as soon as, in case, etc.)

Method

As in Activity 11, at the end of the game the winning student

reads out all five sentences. The student cards are on page 44 and the teacher's board is on page 39.

Jigsaw reading activities

The activities in this section involve various forms of jigsaw reading, from simple broken sentences to the more complicated of putting together of complete stories. They are useful for testing, amongst other things, linking words.

13 Broken sentences 1   *Elementary*

In this activity students have to put together sentences which have been broken up into two halves.

Grammar points

Present simple

Method

1 Copy, cut up and *shuffle* the broken sentences on page 45. Make enough sets for the class working in pairs or groups of three or four.

2 Give each group a set of cards and tell them they have to arrange them into 15 sentences.

3 Set a definite time limit and stop the students at the end of it, *whether they have finished or not*.

4 Check by going round the class from group to group. Each group reads out one sentence. The teacher says whether it is right or wrong. If right, it can be removed from the table (or turned over). The group gets 1 point for each correct answer. If wrong, the group gets no points and, without giving the correct answer, the teacher moves on to the next group.

5 Continue until all the sentences have been correctly read out.

14 Broken sentences 2   *Intermediate*

Grammar points

Tag questions

Method

As Activity 13. This time each broken sentence is a tag question. The sentences are on page 46.

15 Broken sentences 3   *Intermediate*

Grammar points

Past simple; Linking sentences using 'because'

Method

As Activity 13. This time the second part of each broken sentence begins with the conjunction 'because'. The twelve sentences are on page 47.

16 Broken sentences 4

Intermediate/Advanced

Grammar points

Linking sentences using various conjunctions

Method

As Activity 13. This time each broken sentence contains a conjunction, either at the beginning of the first part *(Although, Provided..., etc.)* or at the beginning of the second part *(as soon as..., even though..., etc.)*. There are twenty sentences altogether arranged as A cards and B cards. The A cards are on page 48 and the B cards are on page 49.

17 Broken sentences 5

Intermediate/Advanced

Grammar points

Prepositions after adjectives

Method

As Activity 13. This time each broken sentence contains an adjective followed by a preposition. There are twenty-four sentences altogether. They are to be found on pages 50–51.

18 Broken sentences 6

Elementary/Intermediate

Grammar points

Past tenses; Prepositional phrases (in the country, for three years, etc.); Word order

Method

As Activity 13. This time the students have to put together eight sentences which have been broken up into three parts. The broken sentences are on page 52.

19 Sort out the sentences 1   *Intermediate*

Grammar points

Present simple; Past simple; Word order

Method

As Activity 13, except that his time the students write down their answers rather than manipulate cards. The handout is on page 53.

Key

She prefers dogs to cats – especially poodles.
My uncle works for the BBC as a producer.
We last saw our son in the summer.
They moved to Wales three years ago.

20 Sort out the sentences 2   *Intermediate*

Grammar points

Word order; Present simple; Perfect simple; Prepositional phrases

Method

As Activity 19. The handout is on page 53.

Key

There is too much violence on television.
Everyone over eighteen is allowed to vote.
My wife was trained to be a teacher in Cambridge.
In Britain people still drive on the left.
It isn't warm enough yet to go swimming.

21 Jigsaw reading 1   *Intermediate*

The next three activities consist of getting the students to sort out complete texts rather than single sentences.

Grammar points

Word order; Imperatives as used in instructions for a recipe

Method

1 Copy the handout on page 54 and give each pair a copy.

2 Explain what is to be done and set a time limit.

3 Check orally. For homework, the students could write similar step-by-step instructions for how to do other things, e.g. change a nappy, change a fuse, mend a puncture, etc.

Key

Fill a kettle full of cold water.
Let the water come to the boil, but do not let it go on boiling for any length of time.
Pour some of the water into a teapot to heat it thoroughly.
Pour the water away and put in the tea, one teaspoon per person and one for the pot.

*Take the teapot to the kettle and pour the water onto the tea
while it is still boiling.
Stir briskly, put the lid on the teapot and let it brew for several
minutes.
You will now have a perfect cup of tea.*

---

22 Jigsaw reading 2 *Intermediate/Advanced*

Grammar points

Linking sentences logically

Method

1 Copy, cut out and *shuffle* the parts of the two jokes on pages 55–56. Divide the class into groups of 3–5 students. Give each group a set of cut-up cards.

2 Explain that the groups have to sort out the cards so that they make two jokes. If they need extra help, you can say that there are 14 parts in joke 1 and 15 parts in joke 2.

3 Set a definite time limit and check orally. One student from one group can start with the first part of joke 1, then another student reads out the next part, and so on.

---

23 Jigsaw reading 3 *Advanced*

This activity is more difficult than the others and is meant to be done orally.

Grammar points

Linking sentences logically

Method

1 Copy, cut out and *shuffle* the parts of the story on page 57. Divide the class into groups of 5–8 students. Give each student one or more parts of the story. Tell them they are *not allowed to let anyone else see their card(s).*

2 Explain that they are allowed to read out what is on their card but they mustn't write anything down. The aim is to sort out the story orally in the correct order.

3 Set a definite time limit and stop the students at the end of it, *whether they have finished or not.*

4 Check orally using the same method as in Activity 22.

Acknowledgement: I was first introduced to this type of activity by Mario Rinvolucri on one of his many visits to Sweden.

Asking and answering questions activities

These activities are concerned with asking and answering questions in various forms, from simple Yes/No type questions to more complicated WH- ones.

Questions with short Yes/ No answers

---

24 Yes/No questions 1 *Elementary*

This and the following two activities are simple guessing games for the whole class.

Grammar points

Asking questions (Does he/she…?); Short Yes/No answers + adverbs of frequency (Yes, always, No, never, etc.)

Method

1 Give everyone a copy of the handout on page 58.

2 The teacher can demonstrate first to show the class what they have to do. You think of a person in your family and ask, for example, *What's my uncle's job?*

3 The rest of the class try to guess by asking questions. You can only answer Yes/No (+ adverb) or I don't know/I'm not sure.

4 The game goes on until someone in the class guesses the job or when the class have got **ten** No-answers.

5 When a person guesses, he or she should say: *Is your (uncle) a (doctor)?*

---

25 Yes/No questions 2 *Elementary*

Grammar points

Asking questions (Do you…?, Is it…?); Short Yes/No answers (Yes, I do, Yes, sometimes, No, I don't, No, not usually.)

Method

As Activity 24. The handout is on page 59. This time at the beginning the student asks the class: *What do I like doing in my free time?* When a student guesses, (s)he asks: *Do you like (swimming)?*

26 Yes/No questions 3   *Elementary*

Grammar points

Asking questions (Is this country…?, Do they…?, Is there…?, Are there…?); Short Yes/No answers (Yes, it is, Yes, they do, Yes, there is/are, etc, No, it isn't, No, they don't, No, there isn't/aren't, etc.)

Method

As Activity 24. The handout is on page 60. This time at the beginning the student asks the class: *Which country am I thinking of?* When a student guesses, he or she asks: *Are you thinking of (Greece)?*

27 Yes/No questions 4
Elementary/Intermediate

This activity is for pairs.

Grammar points

Asking questions (Do you…?); Short Yes/No answers (Yes, I do/No, I don't)

Method

1 Copy and cut out the handouts for Student A and Student B on page 61.

2 Divide the class into pairs – A and B. Give each person the appropriate handout.

3 At first they work alone, They read through the sentences and fill in the answers by making guesses about their partner, for example, whether (s)he smokes, enjoys going to discos, etc.

4 When both are ready, they face each other and take it in turns to check if they have guessed correctly or not by asking and answering questions.

5 The partner with the highest number of correct guesses wins.

Role-plays and simulations

The following activities are much freer and make use of WH-questions.

28 Things we were going to do
Intermediate/Advanced

In this simulation, students work in pairs and imagine that their partner is an old school friend.

Grammar points

Was/were going to…; Asking and answering questions (past tenses)

Method

1 Copy and cut out the handouts for Student A and Student B on page 62.

2 Divide the class into pairs – A and B. Give each person the appropriate handout.

3 Explain what they have to do and allow time for preparation before they start.

4 When both are ready, they face each other and begin.

5 Set a definite time-limit and stop the students at the end of it, *whether they have finished or not.*

6 You can follow up by asking the students if they have ever made plans that either came true or didn't come true.

29 Asking and answering questions about photographs
Intermediate/Advanced

In this simulation, students work in pairs and imagine that they are showing their partner some photographs they have taken.

Grammar points

Asking and answering questions (various tenses)

Method

As Activity 28. The handouts and photographs are on page 63. As a follow-up, you can ask the students to bring in 'real' photographs to talk about.

30 My first love   *Intermediate/Advanced*

In this simulation, students work in pairs. One person shows the other a photograph of the first person (s)he fell in love with. His or her partner asks questions about this person.

Grammar points

Asking and answering questions (various tenses)

Method

As Activity 28. The handouts for Student A and Student B are on page 64.

31 Answering an advertisement   *Intermediate*

In this simulation, students work in pairs. Student A wants a third person to share a house and has put an advert in the newspaper. Student B phones up about it.

Grammar points

Asking and answering questions (various tenses)

Method

As Activity 28. The handouts for Student A and Student B are on page 65.

---

32 Group role play   *Intermediate*

This is a role-play for groups of eight students. It is similar to the *Find someone…* activities earlier in the book.

Grammar points

Asking questions (Did you…?); Yes/No answers

Method

1 Copy and cut out the 8 role cards on pages 66–67.

2 Divide the class into groups of eight students. Each student is given a role card.

3 Explain that each person has some information on their card about themselves, but they also need to find out three things about others in the group.

4 Allow time for them to work out which questions to ask. Demonstrate with the whole class, if necessary.

5 When everyone is ready, the role-play can begin. They take it in turns to talk to different people in the group, trying to find out the three missing pieces of information.

6 Set a definite time limit and stop the students at the end of it, *whether they have finished or not.*

Other question and answer activities

---

33 Getting to know you 1   *Elementary/Intermediate*

This and the next activity concentrate on asking questions of a more personal nature. Because of this, it is important to tell the group that they don't have to answer any questions they find too personal.

Grammar points

Asking questions in order to complete a form (various tenses, mainly WH-questions); Reported speech

Method

1 Divide the class into pairs and give each student a copy of the handout on page 68.

2 Students now take it in turns to ask questions and fill in the form.

4 Set a definite time limit and stop the students at the end of it, *whether they have finished or not..*

5 As a follow up, each person finds a new partner and tells him or her one or two things about the person (s)he interviewed.

---

34 Getting to know you 2

Intermediate/Advanced

Grammar points

Asking WH-questions (various tenses)

Method

1 Copy and cut out the handouts for Student A and Student B on page 69.

2 Divide the class into pairs – A and B. Give each person the appropriate handout.

3 Explain what they have to do. Each person works on his/her own and writes down his/her answers on a separate piece of paper. Allow about 10–15 minutes for this.

4 Student A and Student B now turn over their handouts and from now on only use the piece of paper they have written their answers on. They are allowed to refer back to the handout if they can't remember what a particular date or name was but their partner must **not** be allowed to see the handout. They take it in turns to ask about the various names, dates, etc. Encourage them to ask follow-up questions so that their partner talks as much as possible.

5 Set a definite time limit and stop the students at the end of it, *whether they have finished or not.*

---

35 Ask the right question

Intermediate/Advanced

This is an activity for groups of up to eight students.

Grammar points

Asking WH-questions (various tenses)

Method

1 Copy, cut up and *shuffle* the cards on page 70.

2 Divide the class into groups of up to 8 students. Give each group a set of cards. Place them face down on the table.

4 One student begins. (S)he picks up a card and tries to ask a question that will make someone answer with this word. The person who answers, keeps the card (and gains 1 point). The next student picks up a card, and so on.

5 Set a definite time limit. The student with the highest number of points at the end is the winner.

NOTE: A variation would be for the students to play in teams (as in Bridge). Player 1 from team A has 2 minutes to get his partner to answer correctly. If not, Team B can try and guess and thus gain the point

36 Keep talking   *Advanced*

This activity can either be done in groups or as a whole class activity. *(Whole class activity described below.)*

Grammar points

Asking WH-questions (various tenses)

Method

1 Copy, cut out and *shuffle* the 12 cards on page 71.

2 The teacher can demonstrate first by telling the class that (s)he's going to say something and that the class must try and find out as many further details as possible by asking questions. To help them, you could write up on the board the following question words:

   Why? What? Where? When? Who? etc.

3 Take one of the cards (you can choose one which best suits you!) and say it to the class. Encourage them now to ask you as many questions as possible. Stop after about 3 minutes.

4 Ask for volunteers and continue in the same way with the remaining cards.

5 Alternatively, the students could work on their own in groups, taking it in turns to be the person who utters the opening statement. Each group must have a set of cards.

Information-gap activities

These are activities where the students, usually working in pairs, each have access to some information. By working together they try to solve the whole.

37 What are the missing numbers?

Elementary

This activity tests the students' knowledge of numbers, ranging from nought to over a thousand.

Grammar points

Cardinal numbers

Method

1 Copy and cut out the handouts for Student A and Student B on page 72.

2 Divide the class into pairs – A and B. Give each student a copy of the appropriate handout.

3 They sit facing each other, making sure that their handout is hidden from their partner.

4 Explain what is to be done and allow time for preparation. Everyone then starts at the same time.

5 Set a definite time limit and stop the students at the end of it, *whether they have finished or not.*

6 They now compare handouts to see how well they have done.

38 What are the missing dates?

Elementary

This activity tests the students' knowledge of ordinal numbers as used in dates.

Grammar points

Ordinal numbers (from 1st to 30th)

Method

As Activity 37. Both handouts for Student A and Student B are on page 73.

39 Four people   *Elementary*

In this activity, the students try to find out personal information about four people.

Grammar points

WH-questions; Present simple

Method

As Activity 37. The handout for Student A is on page 74 and the handout for Student B is on page 75.

40 A day in the life of Jane Wilson

Elementary

In this activity, the students try to find out how a person usually spends her day.

Grammar points

WH-questions; Present simple; Giving clock times

Method

As Activity 37. The handout for Student A is on page 76 and the handout for Student B is on page 77.

As a follow-up you could get the students to write their own 'typical' day (or weekend) in the same way.

41 Biographies   *Intermediate/Advanced*

In this activity, the students try to find out missing information about the lives of two well-known people from the past.

Grammar points

WH-questions; Past simple

Method

As Activity 37. The handout for Student A is on page 78 and the handout for Student B is on page 79.
As a follow-up you could get the students to write their own mini-biography of someone famous from their country.

Acknowledgement: The biographies are adapted from *Who They Were*, General editor Lesley Firth, published by Kingfisher Books, Grisewood & Dempsey Ltd, 1989

42 It's a fact!   *Intermediate*

In this activity, the students try to complete the missing information in sentences based on amazing facts. Then they work together to decide which of the facts are completely untrue.

Grammar points

WH-questions (various tenses)

Method

As Activity 37. The handout for Student A is on page 80 and the handout for Student B is on page 81.
When they have finished, ask for their suggestions as to which facts are complete lies. (Give the correct answers if necessary.)

Key

The following sentences are completely untrue:
Nos 3, 7, 10, 16 and 19.

43 Holiday plans   *Elementary/Intermediate*

In this activity, the students complete tables showing four people's holiday plans.

Grammar points

WH-questions; Present continuous with future meaning

Method

As Activity 37. The handout for Student A is on page 82 and the handout for Student B is on page 83.
As a follow-up you could get the students to tell you their own holiday plans.

44 A family tree   *Intermediate*

This is a group activity for groups of six students. If there are fewer students, one person will have to have more than one information card.

Grammar points

Use of 's to show possession; Present simple

Method

1 Copy and cut out the handout of the James family tree and the six information cards on page 84. Make sure you have enough copies for each group.

2 Divide the class into groups of six students. Give each student an information card and each group a copy of the blank family tree.

3 The groups sit around a table. One person in the group acts as 'secretary' and is responsible for filling in the blank family tree. Alternatively, each person in the group could have his/her own copy of the blank family tree.

4 Explain what is to be done and set a time-limit.

5 Check orally. (You could draw a blank tree on the board and get the groups to fill it in for you.)

Key

ROW 1:	*Douglas, Sylvia*
ROW 2:	*Sally, Mark, David, Anne, Peter, Nina*
ROW 3:	*nurse, electrician, accountant, editor, teacher, doctor*
ROW 4:	*Amanda, Bob (or Tom), Tom (or Bob), Joanna (or Rebecca), Rebecca (or Joanna)*

45 Mrs Green's fruit & vegetable stall   *Intermediate*

This is an activity for groups of four students. Working together, the students have to work out where various fruit and vegetables are placed on a stall in order to find out where the carrots are.

Grammar points

Present simple; Prepositions of place

Method

As Activity 44. The main handout and four information cards are on page 85.

Key

ROW 1:	*plums, lettuce, apples, sprouts*
ROW 2:	*cabbage, oranges, CARROTS, pineapples*
ROW 3:	*peaches, cucumbers, grapes, potatoes*

Acknowledgement: This is based on an idea from *Mindbenders and Brainteasers* by Gyles Brandreth & Trevor Truran, published by Chancellor Press, 1993.

45 Half a crossword: Irregular verbs   *Elementary/Intermediate*

In this activity, students work in groups of 2–4. One group

is called A and the other B. Each group has an incomplete crossword containing verbs in the past tense. By asking and answering questions, they complete their crosswords.

Grammar points
Irregular verbs (infinitive and past forms)

Method

1 Copy the crosswords on page 86 (Group A) and page 87 (Group B).

2 Divide the class into A and B groups. They sit facing each other. Give each group the appropriate crossword and allow them time to check that they know the infinitive forms of the verbs on their crossword. (Help if necessary.) On no account are they to show the other group their crossword.

3 They now take it in turns to ask for a verb that is missing from their crossword. They simply ask: *What's 3 down? What's 14 across?* etc. The other group answer, e.g. *It's the past tense of bring*, etc.

4 Set a definite time limit and stop the students at the end of it, *whether they have finished or not.*

6 They can now compare crosswords and check to see if they got any verbs wrong.

Acknowledgement: Based on an idea in an article by Elizabeth Woodeson published in *Modern English Teacher* magazine, 1982, published by Modern English Publications.

Find the differences activities

These are activities where the students, usually working in pairs, have to find a number of differences between two drawings, texts, etc.

Acknowledgement: I first came across this type of activity in *Communication Games* by D. Byrne and S. Rixon, published for the British Council in 1979.

47 Find the differences 1

Elementary

In this activity the students try to find the differences between two drawings.

Grammar points

Asking and answering questions (Present continuous); Giving information using the present continuous

Method

1 Copy the handout on page 88 (Student A) and the handout on page 89 (Student B).

2 Divide the class into pairs – A and B. Give each student a copy of the appropriate handout.

3 They sit facing each other, making sure that their handout is hidden from their partner.

4 Explain what is to be done and allow time for preparation. Everyone then starts at the same time.

5 Set a definite time limit and stop the students at the end of it, *whether they have finished or not.*

6 They now compare their drawings to see if they have found all the differences.

48 Find the differences 2

Intermediate

In this activity the students try to find the differences between two accounts of a person's life.

Grammar points

Asking and answering questions (Past simple); Giving information using the past simple

Method

As Activity 47. The handout for Student A is on page 90 and the handout for Student B is on page 91.

49 Find the differences 3

Intermediate

In this activity the students try to find the differences in four people's diaries.

Grammar points

Asking and answering questions (Future tenses); Giving information using the present continuous with future meaning

Method

As Activity 47. The handout for Student A is on page 92 and the handout for Student B is on page 93.

50 Find the differences 4

Intermediate

In this activity the students try to find the differences between two drawings.

Grammar points

Asking and answering questions (various tenses); Giving information using various tenses; Prepositions of place

Method

As Activity 47. The handout for Student A is on page 94 and the handout for Student B is on page 95.

Questionnaires and surveys

The following activities are based on various questionnaires and surveys with the students working in pairs or groups.

51 Habits questionnaire

Elementary

In this activity the students interview each other to fill in a questionnaire about their partner's habits.

Grammar points

Asking set questions using Do you...?; Yes/No answers + frequency adverbs (Yes, always, No, not usually, etc.); Reported speech

Method

1 Copy the handout on page 96 (Student A) and the handout on page 97 (Student B).

2 Divide the class into pairs – A and B. Give each student a copy of the appropriate handout.

3 They sit facing each other, making sure that their handout is hidden from their partner.

4 Explain what is to be done and allow time for preparation. Everyone then starts at the same time.

5 Set a definite time limit and stop the students at the end of it, *whether they have finished or not.*

6 They now find a new partner and talk to him/her about the person they interviewed.

52 Group interviews

Intermediate

In this activity the students work in groups of up to eight people.

Grammar points

Asking set questions using Do you...?; Yes/No answers + frequency adverbs (Yes, always, No, not usually, etc.); Making statements using the present simple, 3rd person, of the type Most people..., Almost everyone..., etc.

Method

1 Divide the class into groups of up to eight students. Give each student a copy of one of the eight handouts on pages 98–100. Explain what is to be done and allow a few minutes for preparation.

2 They now walk around the room interviewing six other people in their group and making a note of the answers they get.

3 Set a definite time limit and stop the students at the end of it, *whether they have finished or not.*

4 As a follow-up they now write down five sentences based on the results they got, using the following pattern. (It can be written on the board).

Most people...
Almost everyone...
Two/Three people...
Only one person...
Hardly anyone...
No one...

53 How often do you do it?

Intermediate

In this activity the students work in groups of six to eight people.

Grammar points

Asking set questions using How often do you...?; Answering using adverbs of frequency; Making statements using the present simple plus adverbs of frequency

Method

1 Copy the handout on the top of page 101. You will need a copy for everyone in the class. Also copy, cut out and *shuffle* the 'frequency' cards at the bottom of page 101 and the 'activity' cards on page 102. Keep them separate as they will be used for different activities. You should have enough sets for every group.

2 Divide the class into groups of 6–8 students. For variation 1 of this activity, give each student a copy of the main handout and one set of activity cards per group. These are placed face down on the table in the middle of the group.

3 Students take it in turns to pick up a card then ask someone how often they do this particular activity. The student answers with an appropriate adverb of frequency. The activity continues with the next person in the group.

4 Set a definite time limit and stop the students at the end of it, *whether they have finished or not.*

5 In variation 2, each group is given a set of 'frequency' cards. Again they are placed face down on the table. This time instead of asking questions, the student makes a statement using the particular frequency adverb, e.g.

I sometimes go out in the evenings.

54 Likes and dislikes questionnaire
Elementary/Intermediate

In this activity the students work alone first, then in pairs.

Grammar points

Making statements about likes and dislikes, using the verbs love, really like, like, quite like, don't really like, don't like and hate; Agreeing or disagreeing, using so do I, neither do I

Method

1 Give each student a copy of the handout on page 103.

2 Working alone, they fill in the questionnaire.

3 When they have finished, they find a partner and have conversations based on the example on the handout.

4 As a follow-up, encourage a general class discussion with the students suggesting other things they like or dislike.

55 Asking about likes and dislikes
Intermediate

This is a slightly more difficult version of the previous activity for pairs.

Grammar points

Asking questions about likes and dislikes; Answering using Yes/No phrases (Yes, very much, No, not at all, etc.); Making statements about a person's likes and dislikes; Reported speech

Method

1 Copy and cut out the handouts for Student A and Student B on page 104.

2 Divide the class into pairs – A and B. Give each student a copy of the appropriate handout.

3 They sit facing each other, making sure that their handout is hidden from their partner.

4 Explain what is to be done and allow time for preparation. Everyone then starts at the same time.

5 Set a definite time limit and stop the students at the end of it, *whether they have finished or not.*

6 They now find a new partner and talk to him/her about the person they interviewed using the pattern on their handout.

56 What sort of a person are you?
Intermediate/Advanced

This is an activity for groups of six.

Grammar points

Making personal statements using the present simple + adverbs of frequency; Reported speech (follow-up activity)

Method

1 Divide the class into groups of six and give each student a different one of the handouts on pages 105–107.

2 Working alone, they fill in column 1 about themselves. As this is personal information tell them they don't have to answer any questions that are too personal.

3 They now take it in turns to interview the other five people in the group, writing down their answers in columns 2–5.

5 As a follow-up you could ask some students to make some generalisations based on their findings, e.g. *Everyone I spoke to said they were honest, No one said they were good with their hands,* etc.

57 Have you ever...?
Intermediate

This is an activity for groups of 5–8 students.

Grammar points

Asking set questions (Present perfect); Speculating; Making statements using All of us..., Most of us..., Only a few of us..., None of us..., etc.

Method

1 Divide the class into groups of 5–8 students. Give each student a copy of the handout on page 108.

2 Working alone, they try to guess how many people in the group have done the various things. They write the number down in the column *How many?*

3 They now work as a group and take it in turns to ask each other questions to find out the exact number who have done each activity. They write this number down in the column *Correct.*

4 Set a definite time limit and stop the students at the end of it, *whether they have finished or not.*

5 They now fill in the missing words *All of us, Some of us,* etc. in front of each statement, based on their results.

6 As a follow-up, go through the twenty statements with the whole class, taking it in turns to ask students from the various groups to read out what they have written.

58 What do you think?

Intermediate/Advanced

This is a teacher-led activity in groups.

Grammar points

General grammar (mainly present simple) especially as used in giving opinions and agreeing and disagreeing with them

Method

1 Divide the class into groups of 6–8 students and give each student a copy of the handout at the top of page 109.

2 Read out the sentences on the teacher's sheet at the bottom of page 109 in order. After you have read each one tell the students to give their opinion by writing a key word (in capitals after each statement) in one of the ten boxes on their sheet. If they write the word in box 1 it means they disagree strongly, while if they write it in box 10 it means they agree strongly. Anywhere in-between shows the strength of their agreement or disagreement.

3 When you have finished, the students will be left with single words written on their sheets. (Very few of them will remember exactly what these words mean.)

4 Ask one group to give you a number between 1 and 15. When they do so, read out that statement again. The people in the groups now show each other where they had placed the word and a short discussion can begin. Encourage them to agree and disagree with each other.

5 Set a definite time limit for this discussion and stop the students at the end of it, *whether they have finished or not.*

6 Carry on with another number chosen by the next group.

7 As a follow-up ask each group in turn which statement caused the most discussion.

Giving and receiving instructions activities

The following activities are based on giving and receiving instructions, with a special emphasis on prepositions of place.

59 Can you follow instructions?

Elementary/Intermediate

This activity is strictly for fun! The students are told they only have five minutes to complete a seemingly complicated handout. However, it is all a bluff and if they follow sentence 1 and read through the questions before starting to write anything, they will find out why. But most students take a while before they realize that all they have to do is write their name at the bottom of the page.

Grammar points

Understanding written instructions; Imperative forms as used in giving instructions

Method

1 Give everyone a copy of the handout on page 110.

2 Read through the instructions emphasising the fact that they only have five minutes in which to complete everything. Make a thing about having pens ready and starting at the same time. Build up the atmosphere so that it feels like a real race against time.

3 Shout *Start!* at which signal everyone begins.

4 Depending on the group, you may or may not need to shout *Time's up!* If you do, draw their attention to the first and last sentences (and hope you don't get lynched!)

5 You can, if you wish, do it as a real exercise, in which case all you have to do is cross out the word 'just' in the last sentence. (The students could even work in pairs.)

60 Complete the drawing

Intermediate

In this activity the students work in pairs. Student A has a complete drawing while Student B's drawing is incomplete. Student A helps B to complete his/her drawing.

Grammar points

Giving instructions (imperatives); Prepositions of place

Method

1 Copy and cut out the handouts for Student A and Student B on page 111.

2 Divide the class into pairs – A and B. Give each student a copy of the appropriate handout.

3 Explain what is to be done and allow time for preparation. Make sure Student A keeps his/her drawing hidden from Student B. Also remind him/her that (s)he is not allowed to point to or touch Student B's drawing.

4 Set a definite time limit and stop the students at the end of it, *whether they have finished or not.*

61 Up, down, left, right 1

Elementary

In this activity one student dictates instructions to another.

Grammar points

Giving set instructions (imperative); Prepositions (in, up, down, left, right, above, below)

Method

As Activity 58, The handouts are on page 112 (Student A) and on page 113 (Student B).
When they check at the end, remind Student B to hide the bottom part of his/her handout. The roles are now reversed, with Student B now giving Student A instructions.

62 Up, down, left, right 2

Elementary/Intermediate

This is a slightly more difficult version of the previous activity.

Grammar points

Giving set instructions (imperative); Prepositions (in, up, down, left, right, above, below)

Method

As Activity 58. The handouts are on page 114 and the top of page 115 (Student A) and at the bottom of page 115 (Student B).

63 Taking a group photograph

Intermediate/Advanced

In this activity for groups of six students, one person tries to arrange the others for a photograph.

Grammar points

Giving instructions (imperative); Prepositions

Method

1 Divide the class into groups of 6. Choose one student as the photographer and give him/her a copy of photo 1 on page 116.

2 Explain what is to be done and allocate space for each group. Set a definite time-limit and stop the students at the end of it, *whether they have finished or not.*

3 The teacher can act as a judge at the end and decide which group is closest to the original. Award points, if you wish.

4 When they have done it once, a new photographer can be chosen and the activity is repeated, this time using photo 2 on page 116.

NOTE: A polaroid camera would be ideal for this activity,
or why not video it?

64 Arrange the furniture 1

Intermediate

This is an activity for groups of four. It needs more preparation than usual and it is a good idea, if possible, for everything to be mounted on card.

Grammar points

Giving instructions (imperatives); Prepositions of place

Method

1 Make one copy of the handout on page 117 which contains the finished layout. Make one copy per group of the handout of the blank room on page 118. Also make copies for each group of the key to the furniture at the bottom of page 119. Finally, cut out and mount on card if possible the various items of furniture at the top of page 119 (again one set per group).

2 Divide the class into groups of four. Give each group a handout of an empty room, a set of furniture and a key to the various cut out objects *(dining table, bookcase, plants, etc.)*

3 The class work at the same time. The teacher places the master layout on his/her desk, with its back to the class. (You can mount it like a photograph.)

4 One person from each group now comes out to the front and is allowed to look at the master layout for 1 minute.

5 Then they go back to their groups and *without touching anything themselves* tell the rest of the group where to place the furniture. (They obviously won't remember everything.)

6 Let a few minutes pass, then get the next person in the group out. Again, they look at the master drawing for 1 minute, then go back to their respective groups.

7 The activity continues until all four students have been out the front. Finally, one student from each group can come out again for a final look.

8 The teacher now goes to each group in turn to see how well they have done. Award them a mark out of 10.

NOTE: Another way of using the cards is for one group to arrange the furniture and then try to get the other group to arrange theirs in the same way, by telling them where to put things.

65 Arrange the furniture 2

Intermediate/Advanced

This is a variation of the previous activity for groups of six students.

Grammar points

Making statements using the present simple + prepositions of place; Imperatives

Method

1 Use the same handouts in Activity 64, namely the empty room plan, furniture cutouts and furniture key. In addition, copy the group cards on page 121 (one set per group).

2 Divide the class into groups of six students. Give each group one copy of the room plan, furniture cutouts and key and each student in the group one of the six group cards.

3 Explain that they can read out what is on their group cards but that they are not allowed to write anything down or show their cards to anyone else. Working together, they try to furnish the room according to the information on their group cards.

4 Set a definite time limit and stop the students at the end of it, *whether they have finished or not.*

5 The teacher now goes to each group and sees how well they have done by checking their final arrangement with the one on page 120. Again each group can be awarded a mark out of 10.

66 The adverb game

Intermediate

This is a whole class activity.

Grammar points

Adverbs of manner; Making statements with going to + verb + adverb of manner

Method

1 Copy, cut out and shuffle the adverb cards on page 122 and the activity cards on page 123.

2 Divide the class into two teams – A and B. Place the adverb cards and the activity cards face down on a table in front of the class.

3 Team A begins. One person comes out the front, turns over the top activity card, plus the top adverb card, e.g.

play the piano   angrily

4 This person now says to the class:

I am going to play the piano angrily.

(S)he now mimes the activity for a few minutes, after which the teacher gives him/her a mark out of ten for the performance.

5 Someone from team B now comes out the front and the next two cards are turned over. The game proceeds as before.

6 The team with the highest score at the end are declared winners.

NOTE: A variation would be for the students to mime the activity and his/her team to guess (a) the activity and (b) how (s)he is doing it, gaining 2 points for guessing the activity and 5 points for guessing the adverb. If the first team guess wrongly, the other team can try and guess and gain bonus points.

67 Trace the route

Intermediate

In this activity the students work in pairs. Student A helps Student B trace a route on a map.

Grammar points

Giving instructions (imperatives); Prepositions of place

Method

1 Copy the handouts on page 124 (Student A) and on page 125 (Student B).

2 Divide the class into pairs – A and B. Give each student a copy of the appropriate handout.

3 Explain what is to be done and allow time for preparation. Make sure Student A keeps his/her drawing hidden from Student B. Also remind him/her that (s)he is not allowed to point to or touch Student B's drawing.

4 Set a definite time limit and stop the students at the end of it, *whether they have finished or not.*

68 The audition

Advanced

This activity is a role play for pairs based on someone auditioning for a part in a television commercial.

Grammar points

Giving instructions (imperatives); Polite requests (Would you…? Do you think you could…? etc.)

Method

As Activity 67, but one person is the producer and the other the actor/actress. The actor/actress will need a pen to make notes on his/her script. The producer's script is on page 126 and the actor/actress's script is on page 127.

As a follow-up, one or two pairs could be asked to 'perform' in front of the class.

Board and card games, etc.

The following activities are based on board games or cards of one sort or another. They should be mounted on card, if possible, so that they can be re-used.

69 20-square 1: Make up a sentence

Intermediate/Advanced

This and the following two activities are based on a board containing 20 squares and are intended for students working in groups.

Grammar points

Making statements using the past tense of irregular verbs

Method

1 Copy the handout on page 129. Make sure there are enough copies for each group. In addition, copy, cut out and *shuffle* the number cards 1–20 on page 128. Again, there should be one set of number cards per group.

2 Divide the class into groups. Give each group the 20-square handout plus a set of number cards. They sit facing each other round a table. The number cards are placed face down on the table next to the handout.

3 Explain that one person picks up a number card, e.g. *Number 7* and looks at the verb in that square, in this case the verb *fly*. (S)he must now make up a sentence using this verb in the past tense, e.g.

Last summer I flew to Spain.

The rest of the group decide whether they will accept the sentence or not. If they do, the verb is crossed out and the student's name is written in this box. Play now continues with the next person.

4 Set a definite time limit and stop the students at the end of it, *whether they have finished or not*. The student with the highest number of 'squares' wins.

NOTE: The reason for using the number cards is that it creates a certain amount of suspense – no one knows which square is going to be next. This usually results in heightened attention.

70 20-square 2: What do you remember?

Intermediate/Advanced

In this activity students have to talk about various things they remember from the past.

Grammar points

General grammar used when talking about the past, predominantly the past simple tense

Method

As Activity 69, but this time they have to tell the rest of the group about the particular item in the square. Encourage the rest of the group to ask further questions to get the person to speak more. The handout to be copied is on page 130.

71 20-square 3: Complete the sentences

Intermediate/Advanced

In this activity students have to complete unfinished sentences.

Grammar points

Completing sentences (various structures)

Method

As Activity 69, but this time they have to think up a suitable ending to a sentence. The handout to be copied is on page 131.

72 Four-in-a-Row: Verbs

Elementary

This activity is for groups of three and tests the students' knowledge of irregular verbs. It is based loosely on the game Noughts and Crosses.

Grammar points

Irregular verbs (3 forms)

Method

1 Copy and cut out the handout on page 132 and the key at the top of page 134.

2 Divide the class into groups of three. Two in the group will compete against one another while the third person will be the referee. Give each group a copy of the handout and give a copy of the key to the referee.

3 Explain what is to be done, namely that students take it in turns to choose a square and then give the three parts of the verb in that square, e.g. for square 23:

freeze froze frozen

The referee checks and then tells the student whether (s)he is right or wrong. If right, (s)he crosses out the verb and writes his/her name in the square. Play now continues with the next person choosing a square and giving the three parts of that verb.

4 Play continues until one student gets a row of four squares – either vertically, diagonally or horizontally.

5 They can now try again with a new copy of the handout

and with someone else being referee.

73 Four-in-a-Row: Prepositions (after adjectives/verbs)

Intermediate/Advanced

This is the same as the previous activity but this time it tests the students' knowledge of prepositions after adjectives and verbs.

Grammar points

Making statements using adjectives and verbs followed by certain prepositions

Method

As Activity 72. The handout is on page 133 and the key for the referee is at the bottom of page 134. This time the student has to add the correct preposition to the verb or the adjective in the square. The referee checks whether the preposition is correct or not.
NOTE: For advanced groups they could be asked to put the word in the square in a sentence together with the correct preposition.

74 The preposition game

Intermediate

This is a board game for groups of four based on various prepositions..

Grammar points

Various prepositions

Method

1 Copy and mount on card, if possible, the board on page 135. Make sure there is one copy for each group. Also copy and cut up the four preposition cards on page 136.

2 Divide the class into groups of four. Give each group a copy of the board plus one of the preposition cards. You will also need enough dice for each group and a counter for each player. Allow time for the students to work out which prepositions are missing from the sentences on their cards. *But they must not write anything at this stage!*

3 Each player starts in one of the *Start here* squares. (S)he must also end in this square.

4 One student begins. (S)he throws the dice then moves his/her counter. In the same throw you are allowed to move in any direction – up, down, left, right or diagonally. You can also combine movements, e.g. if you threw a 6 you could move up 2 squares, left 2 squares then diagonally left 2 squares.

5 Whatever square you land on, you can use that preposition to fill in one of the gaps in your preposition card.

6 The first student to fill in all the gaps and return to his/her home square (they needn't throw an exact number) wins.

7 The teacher can be called in to check the winning card.

75 Ask and tell game

Intermediate/Advanced

This is a board game for groups of 4–5 students.

Grammar points

General grammar (making statements, asking questions)

Method

1 Copy and mount on card, if possible, the board on page 137. Make sure there is one copy for each group. Also copy, cut out and *shuffle* the *Ask* cards on page 138 and the *Tell* cards on page 139.

2 Divide the class into groups of 4–5 students. Give each group a copy of the board plus a set of Tell cards and Ask cards. These are placed face down on the table next to the board. You will also need dice plus a counter for each player.

3 Each player starts in the square marked START. One student begins. (S)he throws the dice then moves his/her counter the appropriate number of squares. If (s)he lands on an Ask square (s)he picks up an Ask card and asks someone else in the group that particular question. If, on the other hand, (s)he lands on a Tell square, then (s)he must tell the others about the particular item on the card.

4 Play goes on in this manner until one or more people land in the END square at the top of the board.

76 Preposition dominoes

Intermediate/Advanced

This is a group activity based on matching verbs/adjectives to the correct preposition.

Grammar points

Various prepositions after verbs and adjectives

Method

1 Copy, cut out and *shuffle* the 75 cards on page 140,

2 Divide the class into groups and each group into two teams – A and B. Give each group a set of cards. Each team gets 37 cards which are placed face down in front of each group. The remaining card is now placed face up in the middle of the table. Let us assume it is the adjective *angry*.

3 Team A begins. They turn up their top card. It can either be a verb, adjective or preposition. Let us imagine they turned up the verb *dream*. They place it next to the word

already on the table.

4 If it is a word that will go with *angry*, namely the preposition *with* or *at* they make up a sentence using their word and group A's word. If accepted, they keep both cards. These are placed to one side. If, as in this case, they turn up a word that doesn't go with *angry* then play moves on to Group B who turn over their top card, e.g. *of* and place it on the table. They see if they can associate any of the words on the table so far. Since you can say *dream of someone/something* they now say what the match is and, with more advanced groups, make up a sentence containing these words. Again, the cards are removed from the table. Play continues in this way.

5 Set a definite time limit and stop the students at the end of it, *whether they have finished or not.*

5 The team with the highest number of cards at the end wins.

NOTE: A variation would be to use the cards to play a game of Memory where pairs of cards are turned up until a match is found.

77 What a question

Intermediate/Advanced

This is an activity for groups of up to eight students

Grammar points

Speculating (conditionals)

Method

1 Copy, cut out and *shuffle* the question cards on page 141 (one set per group).

2 Divide the class into groups and give each group a set of question cards. These are placed face down in the middle of the group.

3 One student starts by turning up the top card, reading it out to the group then saying what (s)he would do. After this, others can say what they would do and a discussion can ensue.

4 The next student now picks up a card, reads it out, etc. The activity continues in this way

5 Set a definite time limit and stop the students at the end of it, *whether they have finished or not.*

6 As a follow-up ask each group in turn which question card gave rise to most discussion.

Acknowledgement: The questions are adapted from those in *The Book of Questions* by Gregory Stock, Ph.D., published by Equation, an imprint of the Thorsens Publishing Group Limited, 1987

Teacher-led activities

In the previous activities in this book the teacher's job has been largely to organise, set up and close an activity, with the students working for most of the time on their own, in pairs or groups. In the following activities, however, the teacher has a more central role but, as before, the students work mainly in pairs or small groups.

78 Countable and uncountable nouns 1

Elementary/Intermediate

This is an activity for the whole class.

Grammar points

Countable and uncountable nouns

Method

1 Copy, cut out and *shuffle* the nouns on page 142.

2 Divide the class into groups. Tell each group that they will need a piece of paper to write down their answers. Tell them to have two columns with the following headings:

COUNTABLE	UNCOUNTABLE

3 Put the pile of cards face down in front of you. Either read them out one at a time or write them on the board. The groups now decide under which column to place the words.

4 Continue until all the words have gone.

5 Check orally.

79 Countable and uncountable nouns 2

Intermediate/Advanced

This is a more advanced version of Activity 78.

Grammar points

Countable and uncountable nouns

Method

As Activity 78. The nouns to be copied and cut out are on page 143.

80 Complete the story 1

Intermediate/Advanced

In this activity the teacher reads out a story with gaps which the students, working in pairs or groups, try to fill in. All the missing words are verbs.

Grammar points

Past simple of regular and irregular verbs

Method

1 Divide the class into pairs or groups of three. Give each pair/group a copy of the handout on page 144.

2 Explain that you are going to read out a story in which twenty-eight verbs are missing. Tell the students that the verbs are the ones on their handout.

3 Read out the story on page 145, pausing after each gap to allow the students to write in their answers.

4 Check orally.

Acknowledgements: This story is adapted from *That's Life,* published by Treasure Press, 1989.

---

81 Complete the story 2

Intermediate/Advanced

This is similar to Activity 80, but this time all sorts of words have been left out of the story.

Grammar points

Filling in missing words in a story (nouns, verbs, prepositions, etc.)

Method

1 Copy and cut up the words on page 146. The first 30 (from *quarrelling* to *fall*) are the words that are missing from the story, while the remaining words are distractors.

2 Divide the class into pairs. Divide the words among the pairs. Make sure each pair has at least one correct word and one distractor.

3 Read out the story on page 147. Pause before each gap and ask for the missing word. The student(s) who thinks (s)he has the missing word, holds it up and says it out loud. If correct, continue with the story. If not, invite other pairs to guess. Further help can be given, if necessary, e.g. *It's a verb. It starts with the letter q.*

4 Continue until all the words have been filled in.

5 As a follow-up, get the students to reconstruct the story again orally from scratch.

Acknowledgement: This story is taken from *Aesop's Fables* retold by Graeme Kent, published by Brimax Books Ltd, Newmarket, 1991.

---

82 Make up a story

Intermediate/Advanced

This is an activity for the whole class. Before starting, divide the class into four groups, A–D. One person in each group will keep the score.

Grammar points

Forming correct sentences (mainly past tense)

Method

1 Copy, cut out and *shuffle* the cards (words) on page 148. Place them face down in a pile on the table in front of you.

2 Take the top three cards and write them on the board, e.g.

dog   yesterday   police

Explain that the aim of the activity is to make up a story, working together as a class.

3 Group A begins. One person starts the story. It can be about anything, but the person (assisted by the group, if necessary) must keep talking until (s)he can use one or more of the words on the board. Once (s)he has, (s)he says *Pass* and the next group continues. Every word used scores 1 point, so in any one turn a group can gain between one and three points. Using the above words, the person migh say, for example,

*I was walking home from school **yesterday** when I saw a strange **dog**. Pass.*   (2 points scored.)

4 Play now passes to Group B. Before they start, wipe out any words used and take new ones from the pack and write these on the board, e.g.

plumber   angrily

NOTE: There should always be three words on the board at any one time..

5 Try to repeat the last sentence (or occasionally summarize the story) as you move from group to group, so the main idea of the story is kept alive.

6 The group with the highest score at the end wins.

NOTE: As a variation, the teacher could select at random 12 words, write them on the board and then get the students, working in pairs or small groups, to write a story around these words. Each pair or group can then read out their story.

---

83 Making comparisons/Finding similarities and differences

Intermediate

This is a game for groups of 3–4 students.

Grammar points

Making comparisons using Both...and, Neither...nor; Comparatives

Method

1 Divide the class into four groups, A–D.

2 Copy set 1 words on page 149 on to the board. Tell the students they have to think of as many things as possible that pairs of words have in common. Give an example, e.g.

Both a guitar and a violin have strings.

You blow both a trumpet and a flute. etc.

Now ask Group A for a suggestion. If correct they get 1 point and play moves on to Group B. Continue with similarities until no one can think of any more. (If a group can't think of anything they say *Pass* and play moves on to the next group.)

3 Now ask them to suggest as many differences as possible between pairs of words, e.g.

A trumpet is lower than a flute.
You play a violin with a bow but a guitar with a plectrum. etc.

Continue as before until no one can think of any more differences.

4 Rub these words out and replace them with another set of words.

5 Continue in this manner until you have gone through all ten sets (or a selection of them).

6 The team with the highest score are the winners.

Acknowledgement: This is based on an idea in *Grammar Practise Activities* by Penny Ur, published by Cambridge University Press, 1988.

---

84 Give an answer 1

Intermediate

This is a written activity for pairs.

Grammar points

Writing sentences (various tenses)

Method

1 Divide the class into pairs and give each pair a copy of the handout at the top of page 150.

2 Explain that you are going to read out ten questions and that they have to think up answers that start with the word *Yes* or *No*. But they also have to give some extra information. Demonstrate, by writing the following on the board.

Are you English?

Yes, I am. I was born in London./But my father is Italian.
No, I'm not. I come from India./But I learnt to speak English at school.

3 Read out the questions on the Teacher's sheet at the top of page 151. Allow time after each one for the students to write down their answers. Remind them that they answer Yes or No but then they must write another sentence with some extra piece of information based on the question.

4 When you have finished, check orally. (Take two or three answers for each question.)

---

85 Give an answer 2

Intermediate/Advanced

This is similar to the previous activity, but this time instead of questions, the teacher reads out a series of statements.

Grammar points

Writing sentences (various tenses)

Method

As Activity 84. The students' handout is at the bottom page 150 and the Teacher's sheet is at the bottom of page 151. Before starting again demonstrate by showing that this time they have to answer using *It's because...* or *That's because...*, e.g.

You sing well.
It's because my mother was an opera singer.
OR That's because I've been having singing lessons for nearly two years. etc.

---

86 The memory game 1

Intermediate

This is a game for pairs.

Grammar points

Answering WH-questions based on a drawing (past simple)

Method

1 Divide the class into pairs. Give each pair a copy of the handout on page 152 and tell them they have five minutes to look at it, trying to remember as much as possible. But they are not allowed to write anything down.

3 Stop them and tell them to turn over their drawings (or collect them). Each pair now writes the numbers 1–15 on a separate piece of paper.

4 Read out the questions on the Teacher's sheet at the top of page 154. Allow time for the students to write down their answers.

5 Check orally. If necessary, they can mark each other's papers. Let them see the drawing again after you have checked.

Key (Suggestion)

1 11:35/23:35/twenty-five to twelve   2 Two   3 No. It was a seascape/a painting of a boat, etc.   4 No   5 A candle/candlestick and a photograph   6 One   7 Yes   8 A vase of flowers and an ashtray ... a newspaper/magazine   9 Behind it 10 Yes   11 Closed   12 No   13 A stereo/record player/CD player, etc.   14 A dog, a cat and a budgie/budgerigar/bird 15 No

87 The memory game 2
Intermediate/Advanced

This is another, slightly more difficult, version of the previous activity based on text items rather than a drawing.

Grammar points

Answering WH-questions based on facts (various tenses)

Method

As Activity 86, but this time the students have to try to remember factual, textual information. You can allow up to ten minutes this time. The students' handout is on page 153 and the Teacher's sheet is at the bottom of page 154.

Key (Suggestion)

1 Your phone calls will be free from then on. 2 You might kill yourself. 3 To see how well they can forge notes. 4 Her watch. Her husband. It was inside a fish he had caught. 5 In US dollar bills. 6 By grabbing its front legs and quickly pulling them apart. 7 Guess exactly how much money (s)he is carrying. 8 By putting them in the freezer overnight. 9 Its eyes pop out. 10 People die and travel around for days. 11 Because they have invented a car that runs on water. 12 They make you look slimmer.

Acknowledgement: These facts are taken from *The Return of Urban Myths* by Phil Healey & Richard Glanville, published by Virgin Books, 1993.

88 What does it mean?
Intermediate

This activity tests the students' knowledge of phrasal verbs. They can work in pairs or groups of three.

Grammar points

Phrasal verbs (various)

Method

1 Copy the handout on page 155 and give each pair/group a copy.

2 Read out the sentences on page 156. Allow a minute or so after each one for the students to write down their answers.

3 Check orally.

89 Explain yourself
Intermediate

This is a game for small groups.

Grammar points

Giving excuses/reasons; Past simple; Clauses using because; Asking WH-questions

Method

1 Copy and cut out the 13 sentences on page 157.

2 Divide the class into small groups.

3 Give a situation to each group. Tell them they now have 5 minutes to come up with a suitable explanation

4 One person from each group gives an explanation. The rest of the class now decide whether to accept it or not. Encourage the rest of the class to interrupt and cross-examine the person talking.

Miscellaneous activities

The remaining activities in the book consist of various handouts, many of which concentrate on writing in one form or another.

90 Complete the sentences 1
Elementary/Intermediate

In this activity the students complete sentences using their own words.

Grammar points

Finishing sentences (mainly present simple)

Method

1 Give each student a copy of the handout on page 158.

2 Each student, working alone, completes the sentences. Tell them that they needn't complete any sentences they find too personal.

3 Set a time limit and stop the students at the end of it, *whether they have finished or not.*

4 They now get together with 2–3 other students in the class and compare their answers. You can demonstrate with a student, e.g. *My least favourite animals are snakes and crocodiles. What about you? What are your least favourite animals?* etc.

91 Complete the sentences 2
Intermediate/Advanced

Grammar points

Finishing sentences (various tenses)

Method

As Activity 90. The handout is on page 159.

92 Complete the sentences 3

Intermediate/Advanced

Grammar points

Finishing sentences (adjective + preposition); Adverbs of frequency

Method

As Activity 90. The handout is on page 160.

93 Complete the sentences 4

Intermediate/Advanced

Grammar points

Finishing sentences (conditionals)

Method

As Activity 90. The handout is on page 161.

94 Right word, wrong place 1

Elementary

This activity tests the students' knowledge of word order, especially their ability to see which two words in a sentence are in the wrong places.

Grammar points

Word order

Method

1 Divide the students into pairs and give each pair a copy of the handout at the top of page 162.

2 Explain what is to be done by reading through the example with the whole class. If necessary, do the first sentence orally.

3 Set a time limit and check orally.

Key

1 pocket, wallet 2 the, near 3 warm, cold 4 quiet, be 5 it, in 6 eight, six 7 Friday, Wednesday 8 work, day 9 tennis, likes 10 vegetables, eats 11 All, the (1st) 12 Piano, she 13 tennis, favourite 14 roof, house 15 films, seen 16 to, likes 17 wide, river 18 exciting, flying 19 Today, it 20 to, go

95 Right word, wrong place 2

Intermediate/Advanced

Grammar points

Word order

Method

As activity 94. The handout is at the bottom of page 162.

Key

1 the (2nd), dog 2 fast, drive 3 we, next 4 unable, ill 5 Was, after 6 Park, they 7 Put, into 8 French, am 9 landing, crashed 10 at, in 11 There, is 12 Grass, keep 13 when, become 14 hair, need 15 on, at 16 like, say 17 it, as (2nd) 18 case, umbrella 19 drawers, forks 20 waiting, kept 21 hoarse, speak 22 Like, do 23 a, there 24 Its, it's 25 into, out

96 Right or wrong 1

Elementary

This is a betting game for pairs or small groups based on deciding whether sentences are grammatically correct or not. Although many teachers are strongly opposed to showing students incorrect sentences, believing students will 'pick up' these mistakes, I have never found it to be the case in twenty years of teaching – especially when the students are told in advance that a sentence may be incorrect.

Grammar points

Deciding whether a sentence is grammatically correct or not (various tenses and structures)

Method

1 Copy the handout on page 163 and give a copy to each pair/group.

2 Explain the rules, namely that for each sentence they put a tick in the right or wrong box and then bet 10–100 points on their answer being correct. They write the number of points in the *Bet* column.

3 Set a time limit and check orally. To avoid cheating, let the students mark one another's handouts.

4 Each answer will either be correct or incorrect. If correct, they gain the number of points they have bet. If incorrect, they lose the number of points they have bet. Students copy the amount under *Bet* to the *Loss* or *Gain* column.

5 At the end, they add up the total losses and gains to arrive at a grand total, which is gains minus losses.

6 The pair/group with the highest score wins.

Key

The following sentences are wrong:
2 (is photography), 3 (her hair cut), 4 (was born), 7 (very well), 8 (tallest), 10 (There are), 12 (borrow), 14 (likes) 15 (How much money)

Acknowledgement: This is a variation of an activity which I first saw demonstrated by Mario Rinvolucri at a workshop in Malmö, Sweden.

97 Right or wrong 2

Intermediate

Grammar points

Deciding whether a sentence is grammatically correct or not (various tenses and structures)

Method

As activity 96. The handout is on page 164.

Key

The following sentences are wrong:
1 (some information), 4 (for three days), 5 (good at), 7 (have one too), 9 (I hope not), 11 (have lived/have been living), 12 (he has arrived home late), 14 (What awful), 15 (remind me)

98 Right or wrong 3

Advanced

Grammar points

Deciding whether a sentence is grammatically correct or not (various tenses and structures)

Method

As activity 96. The handout is on page 165.

Key

The following sentences are wrong:
3 (hasn't finished doing), 4 (who's seventy), 5 (such nice weather), 7 (if you work hard), 8 (anything else), 10 (less cold), 11 (looked lovingly) 13 (is Hyde Park)

99 A life history

Intermediate/Advanced

This is a written activity for pairs or groups of three.

Grammar points

Writing someone's life history (mainly past simple)

Method

1 Divide the class into pairs or groups of three and give each pair/group a copy of the handout on page 166 and the photographs on page 167.

2 Go through the life history of Peter Redman orally, then tell the class that they have to make up a similar life history based on one of the people in the five photographs.

3 Set a time limit, e.g. 20–30 minutes.

4 When you have finished, check orally. One person from each pair/group could read out their life history.

NOTE: This activity could also be done as written home-work.

100 Looking after foreign visitors

Intermediate/Advanced

An activity for pairs or groups of three.

Grammar points

Making future plans (future tenses)

Method

1 Divide the class into pairs or groups of three and give each pair/group a copy of the handout on page 168.

2 Explain what is to be done by reading through the instruction at the top of the handout.

3 Set a time limit. When they have finished, they work with another group and compare the plans they have made.

101 What's the question? 1

Elementary

This and the following two activities concentrate on forming correct questions.

Grammar points

Forming WH- questions (various tenses)

Method

1 Divide the class into pairs. Give each pair a copy of the handout on page 169.

2 Explain what is to be done by going through the examples with the whole class.

3 Set a time limit and check orally.

Key (suggestion only)

1 When can I start work? 2 Which exercise was the hardest? 3 Where did he meet his wife? 4 How much does Margaret weigh? 5 How many times have you seen the film? 6 What did he buy? 7 How did she pay? 8 How much did the car cost? 9 How many people were there at the pop concert? 10 How often does he see his parents? 11 Who are they staying with? 12 Who doesn't like spaghetti? 13 How long did you have to wait for your train? 14 Where does Cathy live? 15 On which floor is her flat? 16 For how long have they gone to France? 17 How far is Hastings from London? 18 How long has Cathy worked here? 19 Why is she upset? 20 Whose wife is called Mandy?

102 What's the question? 2

Intermediate

Grammar points

Forming WH- questions (various)

Teacher's notes

Method

As Activity 101. The handout is on page 170.

Key (suggestion only)

1 Which street did the motorcade turn into at 12.30? 2 Which theatre is on West Jefferson? 3 Who was Jack Ruby? 4 When was President Kennedy assassinated? 5 (Many answers possible) 6 Did the squad cars take long to arrive? 7 When was Oswald first spotted? 8 Why did Jack Ruby shoot Oswald? 9 When is Oswald seen staring out of a first-floor window which overlooks Dealy Plaza? 10 (Many answers possible)? 11 Who was J.D. Tippit? 12 Who is alleged to have killed President Kennedy? 13 From which floor are the shots fired? 14 Where did Oswald work? 15 Were the police looking for a black man?

Acknowledgement: This extract is taken from an article in the *Sunday Express*, April 10 1994

103 Rank order 1

Intermediate

In this and the following two activities, students have to rank things in order of importance, working first alone, then in pairs and finally in groups.

Grammar points

Ranking items on a scale; Use of comparatives when discussing the order of items

Method

1 Give each student a copy of the handout on page 171.

2 Tell each student to choose **twelve** items from the list that they are most afraid of. There is no need to rank them at this stage. They simply put a tick or a cross in the boxes marked *You.* Set a time limit

3 Now everyone works in pairs. Working together, they choose **ten** items from the items they have both chosen. (They may need to compromise.) They mark these in the boxes marked *Pairs.* Again, set a time limit.

4 Finally, they work in groups of 3–4. This time, from their list of eight, they choose **six** items, but this time they try to rank them in order, with 1 being the item they are most afraid of. They mark these in the boxes marked *Group.* Set a time limit as usual.

5 As a follow-up, ask one person from each group to list their choices. (You could even write them up on the board, to see if people share the same fears.)

Acknowledgement: The statements for this activity and activities 104–105 are adapted from *The Book of Tests* by Dr. Michael Nathenson, published by Fontana Paperbacks, 1984.

104 Rank order 2

Intermediate

This time the students have to decide what things really annoy them.

Grammar points

Ranking items on a scale; Use of comparatives when discussing the order of items

Method

As Activity 106. The handout is on page 172.

105 Rank order 3

Intermediate/Advanced

This time the students have to decide what makes a successful marriage.

Grammar points

Ranking items on a scale; Use of comparatives when discussing the order of items

Method

As Activity 106. The handout is on page 173.

106 Can it be true?

Intermediate

This is a group activity where students speculate about various facts, some of which are true while others are completely false.

Grammar points

Speculating (using various phrases, e.g. It's definitely true that…, It might be true that…, It's very unlikely that…, etc.)

Method

1 Divide the class into groups. Give each group a copy of the handout on page 174. Tell them they have to decide which facts are true and which are false.

2 Set a time limit and check orally.

Key

TRUE (1, 2, 4, 5, 7, 9, 10, 13, 14, 16)
FALSE (3, 6 (Gone with the Wind), 8, 11 (dyslexia), 12, 15)

Acknowledgement: The facts are based on those found in *The Book of Lists: The 90s Edition* by David Wallechinsky and Amy Wallace, published by Aurum Press Ltd, 1994.

107 Fill in the missing prepositions

Intermediate

This is an activity which tests the students' knowledge of prepositions.

Grammar points

Prepositions (various)

Method

1 Give each student a copy of the handout on page 175 and tell them to fill in the missing prepositions in the text.

2 Set a time limit and check orally.

3 Next they look at the drawings and put them in the correct order 1–10. Get them to re-tell the story in their own words.

Key

Prepositions:
into ... at ... in ... of ... with ... of ... through ... on ... of ... with ... in ... of ... of ... through ... in ... With ... of ... into ... by ... with ... of ... From ... to ... into ... at ... of ... in ... on ... by ... away

Correct order: 9 – 7 – 10 – 8 – 5 – 2 – 6 – 4 – 3 – 1

Acknowledgement: This extract is taken from Lady with Little Dog Seeks Post *by Denys Parsons, published by Pan Books, 1989.*

108 Sort out the text

Intermediate

This is a jigsaw reading activity.

Grammar points

Putting sentences in the correct order

Method

1 Divide the class into pairs and give each pair a copy of the handout on page 176.

2 Tell them to put the text in the right order.

3 Set a time limit and check orally.

Key

The correct order is:
9 – 13 – 17 – 21 – 1 – 6 – 11 – 15 – 19 – 2 – 8 – 14 – 18 – 3 – 16 – 5 – 20 – 12 – 10 – 7 – 4

Acknowledgement: This extract is taken from Lady with Little Dog Seeks Post *by Denys Parsons, published by Pan Books, 1989.*

109 Twenty questions

Intermediate

This is a quiz for groups.

Grammar points

Putting in question words (various, including preposition + question word)

Method

1 Divide the class into groups and give each group a copy of the handout on page 177. Tell them to fill in the missing question words and then to try to answer the questions.

2 Set a time limit and check orally, first the question words

then the answers.

3 As a follow-up they could make up their own quizzes.

Key

Question words:
1 How 2 On what? 3 What 4 Which 5 With which 6 On which 7 How many 8 Who 9 When 10 Why 11 By what 12 In which/ what 13 To which 14 Whose 15 Where 16 For what 17 In which/what 18 What 19 Where 20 From which/what
Quiz answers:
1 XCI 2 The Richter Scale 3 Licensed to kill 4 Alfred Nobel 5 Tennis 6 Lake Ontario 7 Eleven 8 Neil Armstrong and Buzz Aldrin 9 1957–1975 10 In German the name means 'people's car'. Hitler ordered a car for the people to be made and the Volkswagen was the result. 11 Cassius Clay 12 Lord Of The Flies by William Golding 13 Woodwind 14 Banquo's 15 New Zealand 16 China or porcelain 17 Uruguay 18 Dried fish 19 221B Baker Street 20 Japanese or Chinese

110 Place the adjectives

Advanced

In this activity students have to put adjectives in a sentence in the correct place.

Grammar points

Position of adjectives

Method

As Activity 109. The handout is on page 178. Tell them to put the missing adjectives in the correct places in the sentences.

Key

1 some delicious hot soup 2 a nice hot bath 3 in a small brown plastic bag 4 She had big blue eyes and a warm friendly smile 5 a big fat balding middle-aged man 6 an expensive long white silk evening dress 7 a pleasant intelligent young man 8 A long narrow cobbled street 9 a sentimental old Irish song 10 an old American Western film 11 with lovely long dark wavy hair 12 dreadful boring little man 13 a lovely bright sunny day 14 in a comfortable brown leather armchair 15 a cheap modern one-roomed flat 16 in a small round metal box 17 a flashy new red Japanese sports car 18 a beautiful young blonde Swedish girl 19 by a big black fierce-looking dog 20 a valuable antique Swiss gold watch

111 Place the adverbs

Intermediate

In this activity students have to put adverbs in a sentence in the correct place.

Grammar points

Position of adverbs

Method

As Activity 109. The handout is on page 179. Tell them to put the adverbs in the correct places in the sentences.

Key

*1 I usually visit... 2 I hardly ever watch television ... I
frequently listen to the radio 3 I still don't understand...
4 ...and they have all been Volvos 5 ...and they're both married
6 Have you ever... 7 I'm probably going to... 8 I can hardly
hear... 9 She hasn't even... 10 My brother-in-law hardly
ever... He's always so calm... 11 I disagree with you com-
pletely/I completely disagree... Men are definitely...
12 He always goes... but sometimes reads.../but reads for hours
sometimes... 13 I rarely go jogging... There's never... 14 My
brother occasionally.../Occasionally my brother... 15 and he
also plays... 16 Cathy has just... 17 doing my homework yet.
... I've still got... 18 You'll certainly... 19 I definitely saw...
I'm definitely going to... 20 We always get... 21 don't often...
22 I saw her only yesterday 23 he certainly works... 24 They
are all... 25 plays the piano beautifully... usually comes first*

112 Superlatives

Intermediate/Advanced

This is a group activity based on superlatives.

Grammar points

Asking WH- questions using superlatives

Method

1 Copy, cut out and shuffle the superlative question cards
  on pages 180–181.

2 Divide the class into groups of 6–8 and give each group
  a set of question cards. Tell them to place them face
  down on the table in front of them.

3 They take it in turns to pick up a card and ask someone
  else in the group to answer it.

4 As usual set a time limit. As a follow-up, ask each group
  to tell you the most interesting thing said in their group.

113 Fill in the missing words

Intermediate

In this activity students have to fill in the missing words in
a text.

Grammar points

Filling in missing adverbs, verbs, prepositions, etc. in a text

Method

1 Give each student a copy of the handout on page 182.

2 Tell them they have to fill in the missing words in the
  text. There are 32 words altogether.

3 Set a time limit and check orally.

Key

*1 easiest 2 disliked 3 banned 4 who 5 without 6 demanded
7 were forbidden 8 or 9 was sacked 10 by 11 into 12 that
13 when 14 rang 15 should 16 wearing 17 had to
18 promptly/immediately 19 early 20 until 21 were provided
22 failed 23 could 24 up to 25 In spite of 26 because 27 well
28 so 29 immediately/promptly 30 against 31 to 32 had learnt*

114 Fill in the missing verbs

Intermediate

This is similar to the previous activity but this time it is based
on filling in missing verbs from jokes.

Grammar points

Filling in missing verbs in the correct tenses in a text

Method

1 Let the students work in pairs and give each pair a copy
  of the handout on page 183.

2 Tell them they have to fill in the missing verbs in the
  correct tenses. There are 15 altogether.

3 Set a time limit and check orally.

Key

*1 was sold 2 saved ... laid 3 who's stolen 4 uses 5 bit 6 were
singing/are singing 7 I've been stung ... It's flown 8 feel/I'm
feeling 9 invented 10 rang ... I'm bringing 11 I'll have
12 Have (you) been taking/Did (you) take*

115 This is the news

Intermediate/Advanced

In this group activity students have to decide which items to
include in a news broadcast.

Grammar points

*Choosing items then arranging them in order; Firstly...
Then... After that... Finally...; Passive voice*

Method

1 Divide the class into groups. Give each group a copy of
  the handout on page 184 and explain what they have to
  do. Tell them to write down their final choice.

2 Set a time limit and check orally.

3 Ask each group in turn to read out their list of news
  items.

Part 2

Material
for
photocopying

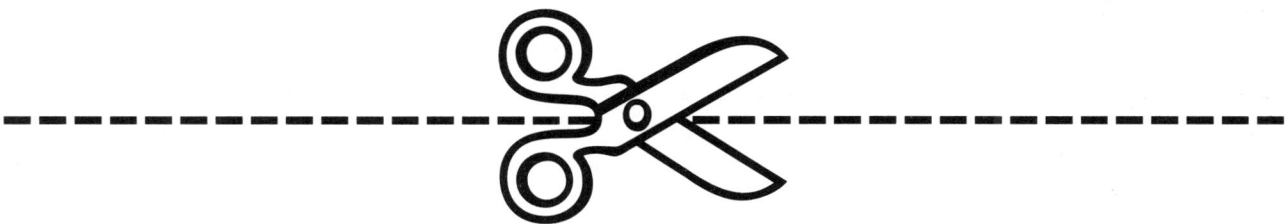

1 FIND SOMEONE WHO...1

1

Find someone:

1 who can ski.
2 who doesn't have a driving licence.
3 who came here today by bus.
4 who has appeared on television.
5 who was born on the same day as you were.

2

Find someone:

1 who can remember what the weather was like last week.
2 who drinks more than six cups of tea or coffee a day.
3 who went abroad last summer.
4 who has never flown.
5 whose father has the same name as yours.

3

Find someone:

1 who can dance the lambada.
2 who doesn't have a telephone.
3 who got up before 7 o'clock this morning.
4 who has been hypnotised.
5 who was born in the same month as you were.

4

Find someone:

1 who can make a funny face.
2 who has a computer at home.
3 who started school before he/she was six.
4 who has never smoked or drunk alcohol.
5 whose mother is the same age as yours.

5

Find someone:

1 who can do a handstand.
2 who doesn't have any brothers or sisters.
3 who went to bed late last night.
4 who has been in love more than five times.
5 who was not born in hospital.

6

Find someone:

1 who can't whistle.
2 who feels faint at the sight of blood.
3 who got married less than two years ago.
4 who has been to Wales.
5 who has the same number of brothers and sisters as you.

7

Find someone:

1 who can hum the British National Anthem.
2 who doesn't want to get married.
3 who was born in a village.
4 who has been skiing recently.
5 who started school at the same age as you did.

8

Find someone:

1 who can't swim.
2 who looks forward to going to the dentist.
3 who hated school.
4 who has been to Moscow or Copenhagen.
5 who has the same interests as you have.

9

Find someone:

1 who can sound like a chicken.
2 who doesn't like watching sport.
3 who was born in January.
4 who has never been abroad.
5 whose favourite pop group is the same as yours.

10

Find someone:

1 who can read music.
2 who has an exciting hobby.
3 who didn't watch TV last night.
4 who has had more than three different jobs.
5 who doesn't usually read a daily newspaper.

Find someone: **11**

1 who can spell his/her name backwards. _____
2 who has relatives in Britain. _____
3 who bought a car last year. _____
4 who has worked in a restaurant. _____
5 who thinks learning English is easy. _____

Find someone: **12**

1 who can speak more than two foreign languages. _____
2 who has more than four brothers and sisters. _____
3 who liked cabbage as a child. _____
4 who has never been in love. _____
5 whose husband/wife/partner is a foreigner. _____

Find someone: **13**

1 who can skate backwards. _____
2 whose brother or sister works in a hospital. _____
3 whose father or mother worked in a bank. _____
4 who has been learning English for more than 6 years. _____
5 who wants to be famous. _____

Find someone: **14**

1 who can use a word processor. _____
2 who thinks he/she is shy. _____
3 who learnt more than one foreign language at school. _____
4 who has never eaten Chinese food. _____
5 who would know how to give the 'kiss of life'. _____

Find someone: **15**

1 who can wake up without an alarm clock. _____
2 who feels sick when people are smoking nearby. _____
3 who grew up in a large city. _____
4 who has been inside the Tower of London. _____
5 who takes the same size in shoes as you do. _____

Find someone: **16**

1 who can wink with both eyes. _____
2 who thinks he's/she's a good cook. _____
3 who used to bite his/her nails. _____
4 who has read a book by Jeffrey Archer. _____
5 who would like to change his/her job. _____

Find someone: **17**

1 who can understand Swedish or Dutch. _____
2 who has never flown. _____
3 who smoked a cigarette just before this lesson. _____
4 who has made more than two speeches in public. _____
5 who thinks babies are boring. _____

Find someone: **18**

1 who can guess what your favourite colour is. _____
2 who thinks he/she is stubborn. _____
3 who saw his/her grandparents last weekend. _____
4 who has stopped smoking recently. _____
5 who can raise one eyebrow. _____

Find someone: **19**

1 who can touch his/her toes. _____
2 who thinks he/she is romantic. _____
3 who walked here today. _____
4 who has moved into a new house or flat recently. _____
5 who can guess how much you weigh. _____

Find someone: **20**

1 who can say 'I love you' in more than three languages. _____
2 who is left-handed. _____
3 who first fell in love when he/she was 15 or 16. _____
4 who has spoken to or shaken hands with a famous person. _____
5 whose hobby is golf. _____

2 FIND SOMEONE WHO...2

Find someone:

1 who thinks he's/she's a good cook.
   (Find out his or her "speciality".)

   _____

2 who belongs to a club or a society.
   *(Find out what sort of club or society
   it is.)*

   _____

3 who collects something as a hobby.
   (Find out what.)

   _____

4 who reads a daily newspaper.
   (Find out which one.)

   _____

5 who remembers his or her dreams.
   *(Find out what a typical dream is
   about.)*

   _____

6 who usually goes to bed late.
   (Find out what time.)

   _____

7 who has a pet.
   *(Find out what sort and if it has a
   name.)*

   _____

8 who watches satellite television.
   *(Find out his or her favourite
   program.)*

   _____

9 who has more than three forenames.
   (Find out what they are.)

10 who likes reading books.
   (Find out his or her favourite author.)

   _____

11 who has a relative who lives abroad.
   (Find out in which country.)

   _____

12 who is not 100% happy with his/her
   body.
   *Find out which part he or she doesn't
   like.)*

   _____

13 who knows a joke in English.
   (Get him or her to tell it to you.)

   _____

14 who lives in a flat.
   *Find out how big it is and what
   his or her neighbours are like.)*

   _____

15 who plays a musical instrument.
   (Find out what.)

   _____

16 who believes in love at first sight.
   *(Find out what sort of person he or
   she is attracted to.)*

   _____

17 who can imitate Donald Duck.
   (Ask for a demonstration!)

   _____

18 who buys clothes at least once a
   month.
   *(Find out what his or her favourite
   colour is and what size shoes he or
   she takes.)*

3   FIND SOMEONE WHO…3

Find someone:

1 who has been abroad more than five times.
(Find out the first foreign country he or she visited.)

2 who had a holiday job when he/she was a student.
(Find out where he or she worked and what he or she did there.)

3 who has ever read a book by Graham Greene.
(Find out what it was called and what he or she thought of it.)

4 who has been to London.
(Find out what they liked most and hated most about it.)

5 who has lived in his/her present address for more than 6 years.
(Find out when he or she moved there.)

6 who has done something for charity.
(Find out what he or she did and how much money was raised.)

7 who has been on a diet.
(Find out what sort of diet and how much weight he or she lost.)

8 who has always wanted to be famous.
(Find out who his or her idol was when he or she was a teenager.)

9 who has been in love more than three times.
(Find out who he or she first fell in love with.)

10 who has been to university.
(Find out where and what he or she studied.)

11 who met his/her partner *(husband, wife, girlfriend, etc.)* less than five years ago.
(Find out where they met.)

12 who has had more than four different jobs.
(Find out what his or her present job is and how long he or she has had it.)

13 who has changed a baby's nappy.
(Ask him or her to mime what he or she did.)

14 who has been frightened or moved to tears by a film.
(Find out which film and why it was so frightening or moving.)

15 who was punished at school.
(Find out what for and what the punishment was.)

16 who has seen a ghost or a flying saucer.
(Find out when and what happened.)

4   IS IT TRUE OR FALSE?

Is it true or false that:

1 more than three people in the group have visited Rome?
2 at least four people watched the news on TV last night?
3 no one was born in June?
4 more than two people are going out tonight?
5 only two people have a car?
6 at least half the group used to smoke (but don't now)?
7 only one person likes getting up early?
8 someone in the group thinks he/she is good-looking?
9 most of the group have had a cold this year?
10 the average weight of the men/women *(choose)* in the group is 74 kilos *(men)*/60 kilos *(women)*?

Use these boxes to fill in names/details, etc.

Q 1	Q 6
Q 2	Q 7
Q 3	Q 8
Q 4	Q 9
Q 5	Q 10

5 FIND OUT LIKES AND DISLIKES

1

You like going to the dentist, but you don't like pop music.

Find out: Name

  1 who likes singing in the shower.   _____

  2 who doesn't like meat.   _____

2

You like Indian food, but you hate flying.

Find out: Name

  1 who loves doing homework.   _____

  2 who doesn't like cats.   _____

3

You like singing in the shower, but you hate the smell of cigarettes.

Find out: Name

  1 who likes going to the dentist.   _____

  2 who doesn't like opera.   _____

4

You love the smell of cigars, but you don't like cats.

Find out: Name

  1 who likes Indian food.   _____

  2 who hates the smell of fish.   _____

5

You like chocolate ice-cream, but you hate getting up early.

Find out: Name

  1 who loves the smell of cigars.   _____

  2 who doesn't like pop music.   _____

6

You like learning English, but you don't like opera.

Find out: Name

  1 who likes going to parties.   _____

  2 who hates flying.   _____

7

You like going to parties, but you don't like meat.

Find out: Name

  1 who likes chocolate ice-cream.   _____

  2 who hates the smell of cigarettes.   _____

8

You love doing homework, but you hate the smell of fish.

Find out: Name

  1 who likes learning English.   _____

  2 who hates getting up early.   _____

6 TRIVIA SEARCH

You know the following: **1**

- When a gorilla is angry it will stick its tongue out at you.
- Dolphins sleep with one eye open all the time.
- Chewing gum while peeling onions will keep you from crying.

You want to know:

1. which was the first country to elect a female Member of Parliament.
2. how to tell if a person is right-handed or left-handed.
3. what is different about telephone directories in Iceland.

You know the following: **4**

- A python can go for as long as a year without eating.
- In ancient Greece a woman's age was counted from the first day of her marriage.
- Finland was the first country to have a female Member of Parliament in 1907, when nine women were voted in.

You want to know:

1. how to find out whether a mosquito is male or female.
2. a way to stop you crying when peeling onions.
3. how the famous Greek writer Aeschylus was killed.

You know the following: **2**

- In Tibet, when guests arrive at your house you greet them by sticking your tongue out at them.
- The average new-born baby spends 113 minutes a day crying.
- The great Greek writer Aeschylus is said to have been killed when an eagle dropped a tortoise on his head.

You want to know:

1. when and where driving licences were made compulsory.
2. what a gorilla does when it is angry.
3. which creature can crawl over a razor blade without cutting itself.

You know the following: **5**

- People in Iceland are listed in the telephone directories by their first names, not their surnames.
- The first driving licences were made compulsory in Paris in 1893.
- The flag of Italy was designed by Napoleon Bonaparte.

You want to know:

1. why in ancient Greece it was very difficult to know how old a woman really was.
2. what happens to you just before you are struck by lightning.
3. how dolphins usually sleep.

You know the following: **3**

- You can find out whether a mosquito is male or female by letting it land on you. If it bites you, it's female.
- It is not unusual to see a woman smoking a cigar in Denmark.
- Just before you are struck by lightning, all the hair on your head will stand on end.

You want to know:

1. how long a new-born baby spends crying every day.
2. an unusual way of finding out an elephant's approximate height.
3. how long a python can live without food.

You know the following: **6**

- If you measure the distance around an elephant's foot and double it, you will find out its approximate height.
- A snail can crawl over a razor blade without cutting itself.
- You can generally tell if a person is right-handed or left-handed by which foot they put into their trousers first.

You want to know:

1. how people in Tibet usually greet guests.
2. who designed the flag of Italy.
3. what is a fairly common sight in Denmark.

7 GROUP OPINIONS

Find out how many in the group:

	1	2	3	4	5	6	7	8
don't trust politicians.								
prefer tea to coffee.								
have never broken the law.								
are allergic to something.								
wish they were ten years younger.								
feel couples should live together before they get married.								
believe in some sort of God.								
think war can never be justified.								
never go abroad on holiday.								
get depressed in the winter.								
worry about losing their job.								
think they are overweight.								

Then report back with:

All of us _____

Most of us _____

Many of us _____

Some of us _____

A few of us _____

Not many of us _____

Hardly any of us _____

None of us _____

8 WHAT'S THE TIME BINGO (teacher's board)

1:00	1:20	2:05	2:50	3:15
3:45	4:10	4:35	5:25	5:55
6:30	6:40	7:00	7:15	8:30
9:25	9:35	10:10	11:55	12:35

9 IRREGULAR VERBS BINGO (teacher's board)

begin BEGAN begun	bite BIT bitten	break BROKE broken	bring BROUGHT brought	buy BOUGHT bought
catch CAUGHT caught	do DID done	drink DRANK drunk	eat ATE eaten	fly FLEW flown
forget FORGOT forgotten	go WENT gone	leave LEFT left	lie LAY lain	run RAN run
show SHOWED shown	sing SANG sung	sleep SLEPT slept	swim SWAM swum	write WROTE written

10   TELEPHONE NUMBER BINGO (teacher's board)

103231	**117720**	**148720**	**189480**	**215088**
253865	**345578**	**346445**	**423518**	**441005**
472552	**501447**	**650381**	**690931**	**720305**
740540	**830451**	**843230**	**866035**	**977420**

11   PREPOSITIONS BINGO (teacher's board)

about	across	at	behind	between
by	down	for	from	in
into	next to	of	off	on
over	through	under	to	with

12 CONJUNCTIONS BINGO (teacher's board)

although	as	as soon as	as long as	because
even if	even though	in case	in spite of	once
provided that	so that	that	unless	until
whatever	when	whenever	whether	while

8 WHAT'S THE TIME BINGO (students' cards)

CARD 1

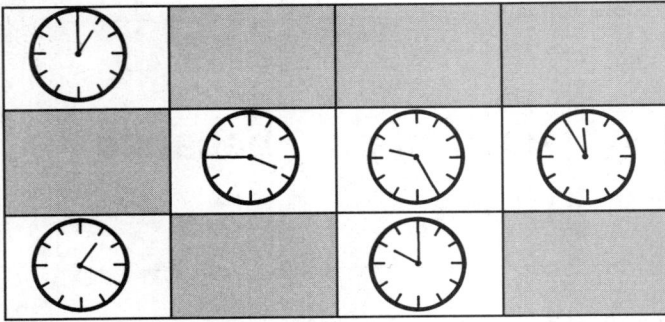

CARD 2

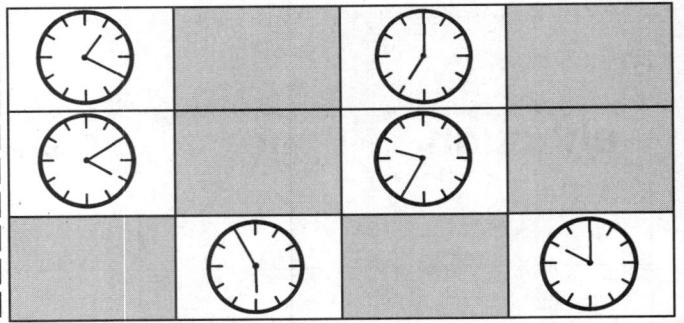

CARD 3

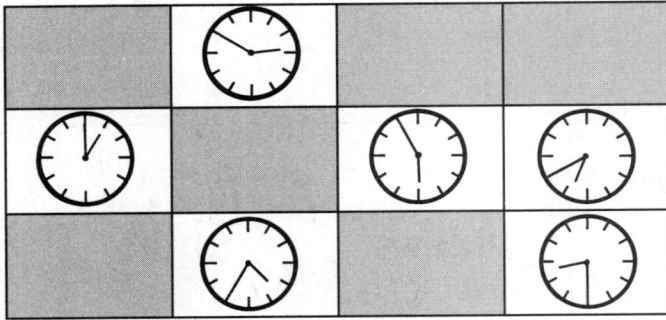

CARD 4

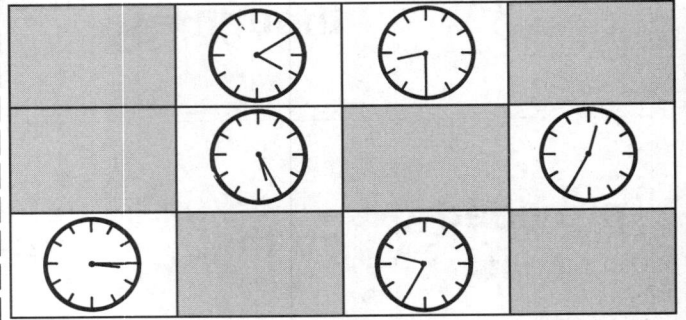

CARD 5

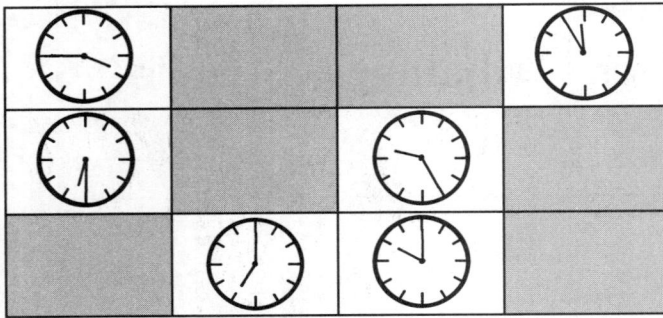

CARD 6

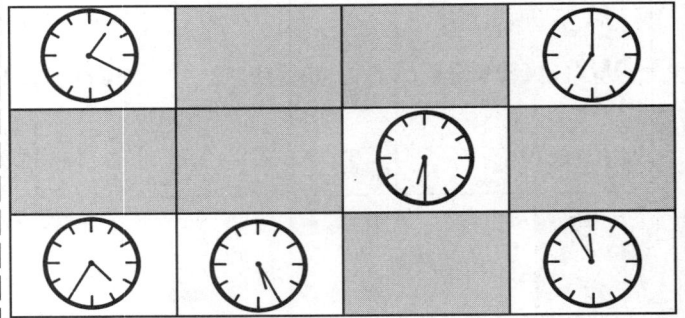

CARD 7

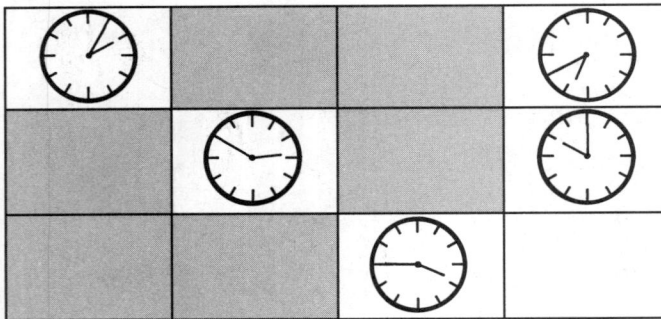

CARD 8

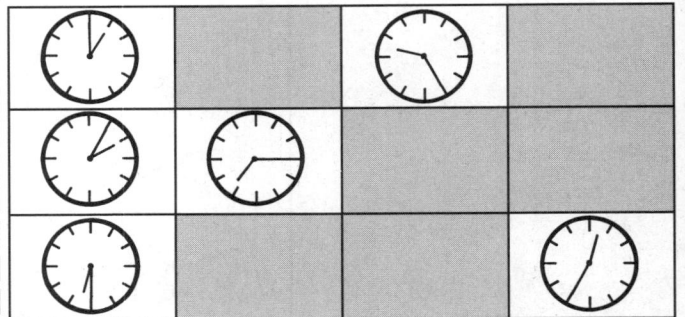

CARD 9

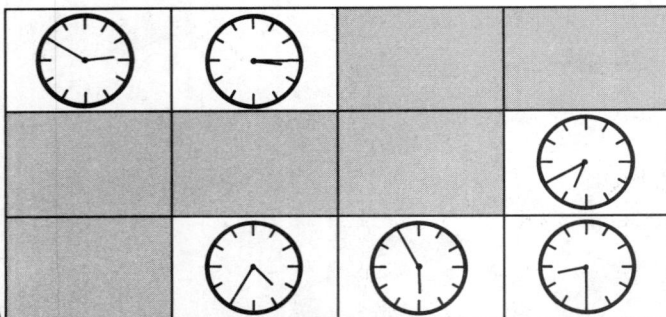

CARD10

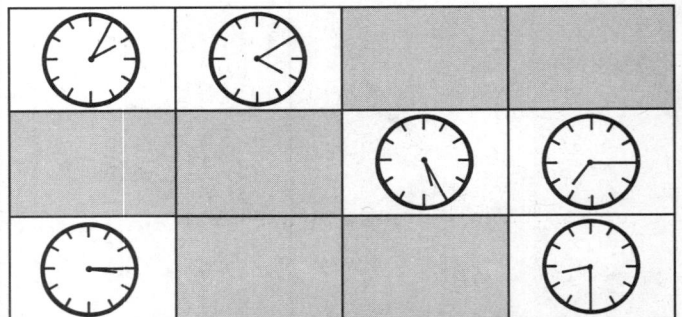

9 IRREGULAR VERBS BINGO (students' cards)

CARD 1

begin			
	catch	show	swim
bite		sleep	

CARD 2

bite		leave	
do		sing	
	fly		sleep

CARD 3

	bring		
begin		fly	go
	drink		run

CARD 4

	do	run	
	eat		write
buy		sing	

CARD 5

catch			write
forget		sing	
	leave	sleep	

CARD 6

bite			leave
		forget	
drink	eat		swim

CARD 7

break			go
	bring		sleep
		catch	swim

CARD 8

begin		show	
break	lie		
forget			write

CARD 9

bring	buy		
			go
	drink	fly	run

CARD 10

break	do		
		eat	lie
buy			run

41

10 TELEPHONE NUMBERS BINGO (students' cards)

CARD 1

103231			
	253865	720305	866035
117720		843230	

CARD 2

117720		650381	
345578		830451	
	441005		8432330

CARD 3

	189480		
103231		441005	501447
	346445		720305

CARD 4

	345578	740540	
	423518		977420
215088		830451	

CARD 5

253865			977420
472552		830451	
	650381	843230	

CARD 6

117720			650381
		472552	
346445	423518		866035

CARD 7

148720			501447
	189480		843230
		253865	866035

CARD 8

103231		740540	
148720	690931		
472552			977420

CARD 9

189480	215088		
			501447
	346445	441005	720305

CARD 10

148720	345578		
		423518	690931
215088			720305

42

11 PREPOSITIONS BINGO (students' cards)

CARD 1

1 Tell me something _____ yourself.
2 I'll see you _____ 8 o'clock.
3 Shall we go out _____ Friday?
4 He was born _____ September.
5 We swam _____ the river to the other side.

CARD 2

1 Tears ran _____ her cheeks as she said goodbye to her friend.
2 Which company do you work _____?
3 He dived _____ the water.
4 I am very proud _____ my country.
5 The boy jumped _____ the wall.

CARD 3

1 The sun went _____ a cloud.
2 Tunbridge Wells is _____ Hastings and London.
3 Do you go to work _____ car?
4 He broke his leg when he fell _____ the stairs.
5 What did you buy your mother _____ her birthday?

CARD 4

1 The children hid _____ the bed.
2 Shall I go with you _____ the station?
3 They bought a house _____ a very big garden.
4 Are you doing anything _____ the weekend?
5 She was born _____ December 10th.

CARD 5

1 He comes _____ Canada.
2 There was silence when the teacher walked _____ the room.
3 The chemist is _____ the library.
4 This door is made _____ steel.
5 Please take your feet _____ the chair.

CARD 6

1 We don't go to school _____ the summer.
2 Don't look round, but the person standing _____ you is the new boss.
3 Is it expensive to travel _____ train in your country?
4 I'm looking _____ my pen. Have you seen it?
5 I got a letter _____ my cousin in Scotland today.

CARD 7

1 There is a bridge _____ the river.
2 They walked home _____ the park.
3 He was wearing a vest _____ his shirt.
4 I always drive _____ work.
5 Have a biscuit _____ your coffee.

CARD 8

1 She sat _____ me at the theatre.
2 He was laughing so much that he fell _____ his chair.
3 The postman pushed the letter _____ the letterbox.
4 What time do you usually go _____ school?
5 Would you like to come _____ me to the cinema tonight?

CARD 9

1 My uncle talks _____ golf all the time.
2 I always have a party _____ my birthday.
3 She walked _____ the street.
4 The post office is _____ the bank and the cinema.
5 The piece of music is _____ Beethoven.

CARD 10

1 Children in this country start school _____ the age of five.
2 My flat is _____ the third floor.
3 Are you interested _____ pop music?
4 "I will love you _____ ever!" he said to her.
5 I don't like stories _____ sad endings.

12 CONJUNCTIONS BINGO (students' cards)

CARD 1

1 We still went to the beach _____ the sun wasn't shining.
2 We decided to go home _____ it was getting very late.
3 I phoned her _____ I found her telephone number.
4 I'll lend you the money _____ you pay me back soon.
5 I wouldn't marry him _____ he was the last man on Earth!

CARD 2

1 He got the sack _____ he kept turning up late for work.
2 _____ he'd asked me I wouldn't have gone. I hate opera!
3 She'll be very attractive _____ she's lost all that weight.
4 We'll go to the beach _____ the weather stays fine.
5 She arrived early _____ she could help me prepare the meal.

CARD 3

1 She was late for work _____ her car broke down.
2 He bought it _____ it was more than he could really afford.
3 Take an umbrella with you _____ it rains.
4 Beethoven composed great music _____ being deaf.
5 You'll be able to play the guitar _____ you have a few lessons.

CARD 4

1 She was so upset _____ she burst into tears.
2 I won't come _____ David and Peter come too.
3 We waited patiently _____ the taxi arrived.
4 _____ you do, James, don't mention the party. It's a secret.
5 Some people like classical music _____ others prefer pop music.

CARD 5

1 I'll lend you my car _____ you fill it up with petrol.
2 He put on his glasses _____ he could see the board better.
3 The film was so boring _____ I fell asleep.
4 The company will go bankrupt _____ we get a big order soon.
5 She was very happy _____ she met Robert Baker.

CARD 6

1 _____ she was very bored, she tried to look interested.
2 There was a loud explosion _____ the bomb went off.
3 We'll book a holiday _____ the new brochure arrives.
4 I'll babysit for you _____ you're back by midnight.
5 I'll take some sandwiches with me _____ I get hungry.

CARD 7

1 Try to be nice to her _____ you think of her in private.
2 I was just getting into the bath _____ the phone rang.
3 I don't care _____ she comes to the party or not.
4 Many people throw away clothes _____ others have nothing to wear.
5 She didn't send for the doctor _____ she was feeling really ill.

CARD 8

1 He couldn't come to the reunion _____ he was abroad at the time.
2 She married him _____ she didn't really love him.
3 _____ his age, he was still a very good tennis player.
4 We'll go for a picnic _____ it doesn't rain.
5 We used to get punished _____ we arrived late for school.

CARD 9

1 There was an unexpected hush _____ the Queen entered the hall.
2 We'll leave _____ John and Pat get here.
3 He carried on playing _____ his knee was hurting him.
4 I took my Visa card with me _____ I bought something.
5 The Beatles wrote wonderful songs _____ not being able to read music.

CARD 10

1 You can't leave the table _____ you've eaten all your food!.
2 He was standing at the bus stop _____ the accident happened.
3 She used to cry _____ she heard the song her ex-husband used to sing to her.
4 It doesn't bother me _____ we go out tonight or not.
5 _____ I was visiting Brighton, I decided to call on an old friend.

13   BROKEN SENTENCES 1

The train usually…	…leaves at 7 o'clock.
She usually gets up…	…at 6.30.
He never has…	…toast for breakfast.
We often go out…	…in the evening.
I speak…	…French and German.
We sometimes have lunch…	…at a Chinese restaurant.
We seldom listen to…	…the radio.
They usually go abroad…	…for their holiday.
Tom and Peter never do…	…their homework.
You never tell me…	…you love me!
Mary sometimes plays…	…tennis on Fridays.
Robert usually meets…	…his friends after work.
My wife and I always watch…	…TV at the weekend.
I hardly ever drink…	…milk or Coca-Cola.
He always wears…	…jeans and a T-shirt.

14 BROKEN SENTENCES 2

It isn't cold,…	…is it?
You stole it,…	…didn't you?
It's Friday today,…	…isn't it?
You didn't say that,…	…did you?
You've got two brothers,…	…haven't you?
They're not French,…	…are they?
They're working hard,…	…aren't they?
He's spoken to her,…	…hasn't he?
He had broken his leg,…	…hadn't he?
He loves you,…	…doesn't he?
You were lying,…	…weren't you?
He wasn't at home,…	…was he?
It's happened before,…	…hasn't it?
You won't tell anyone,…	…will you?
You will do it,…	…won't you?

15   BROKEN SENTENCES 3

I stayed in…	…because I wanted to wash my hair.
I had to use my credit card…	…because I didn't have enough money on me.
I had to get a taxi home…	…because I'd missed the last bus.
I switched on the central heating…	…because the room was cold.
I drew the curtains…	…because it was starting to get dark.
I drank two glasses of water…	…because I was very thirsty.
I went to the local shop…	…because I had run out of bread and milk.
I couldn't get in…	…because I had lost my keys.
I ate a large meal…	…because I was very hungry.
I was late for work…	…because my car broke down.
I didn't phone Julie…	…because I forgot.
I didn't marry him…	…because I didn't love him enough.

Although he was rich…

As it was raining…

We'll go out…

As long as she got well paid…

Because she didn't have a car…

I wouldn't go out with her…

I'll give you £5…

He's a marvellous painter…

Take a torch with you…

We went for a swim…

She'll be an excellent teacher…

Provided that they don't do anything stupid…

I couldn't lend him any money…

He bought a new suit…

It was so cold…

Unless he arrives soon…

Everyone has to die…

Whatever you do, James…

When it rains a lot…

I always feel like dancing…

| ...he lived a relatively simple life. |
| ...they cancelled the picnic. |
| ...as soon as it stops raining. |
| ...she didn't mind what she had to do. |
| ...she could afford to go by taxi more often. |
| ...even if you paid me. |
| ...if you do me a favour. |
| ...in spite of being almost blind. |
| ...in case it gets dark. |
| ...even though the water was freezing. |
| ...once she's had a bit more experience. |
| ...they should win tonight's match easily. |
| ...since I was practically broke myself. |
| ...so that he could make a good impression. |
| ...that the lake froze. |
| ...we'll have to go without him. |
| ...whether they like it or not. |
| ...don't upset her! |
| ...my roof starts to leak. |
| ...whenever I see a Fred Astaire film. |

He was delighted…	…with his present.
She was worried…	…about the exam.
She was always kind…	…to animals.
He was rude…	…to his grandmother.
He was fed up…	…with the bad weather.
We were shocked…	…at the news.
She wasn't satisfied…	…with her exam results.
He is afraid…	…of spiders and snakes.
She was ashamed…	…of her parents.
We are proud…	…of our country.
He was jealous…	…of my success.
I was suspicious…	…of his intentions.

17 BROKEN SENTENCES 5 (continued)

I'm not very good…	…at maths.
My sister is married…	…to an Australian.
He was sorry…	…for his bad behaviour.
This country is famous…	…for its lakes.
She is responsible…	…for the mess.
I'm very interested…	…in tennis.
She's very fond…	…of children.
They were tired…	…of waiting.
Your dress is similar…	…to mine.
Your answer is different…	…from mine.
The room was crowded…	…with people.
I can't pay. I'm short…	…of money.

He bought…	…a house…	….in the country.
She has played…	…the guitar…	….for three years.
I took…	…a taxi…	…to the airport.
We made…	…bacon and eggs…	…for breakfast.
They walked…	…their dog…	…in the park.
He left…	…home…	…two years ago.
I borrowed…	…this book…	…from the library.
They had…	…a biscuit…	…with their coffee.

19   SORT OUT THE SENTENCES 1

Sort out the four sentences.

She	moved	works	our	cats –	years	a producer.
My	prefers	saw	Wales	son	in	ago.
We	uncle	to	to	the BBC	especially	the summer.
They	last	dogs	for	three	as	poodles.

Write your answers here:

1 _____

2 _____

3 _____

4 _____

20   SORT OUT THE SENTENCES 2

Sort out the five sentences.

There	Britain	trained	is	yet	on	Cambridge.
Everyone	is	warm	still	allowed	in	television.
My wife	isn't	too	enough	a teacher	to	left.
In	was	eighteen	much	drive	to go	vote.
It	over	people	to be	violence	on the	swimming.

Write your answers here:

1 _____

2 _____

3 _____

4 _____

5 _____

HOW TO MAKE A NICE CUP OF TEA

Work in pairs. The words in the sentences below are in the wrong order. Put them in the right order. (The commas and full stops are in the correct places.) When you have done that, mark the sentences 1–7 so that they give you step-by-step instructions on how to make tea in Britain.

☐ Pour the water away _____
put in   per person   and   one teaspoon   the tea,   and   for the pot.   one

☐ Stir briskly, put _____
several minutes.   the lid   for   teapot   on the   let it brew   and

☐ Fill _____
cold   full   water.   of   a kettle

☐ You will _____
a   cup of tea.   now   perfect   have

☐ Pour some of _____
a teapot   the water   heat it   into   thoroughly   to

☐ Take the teapot _____
and   while   to the kettle   pour   onto   still   it is   boiling.   the water   the tea

☐ Let the water _____
go on boiling   come   for   to the boil,   do not   but   any length of time.   let it

22 JIGSAW READING 2: SORT OUT THE TWO JOKES

Joke 1

Two old men who lived in a village deep in the country
decided one day to take a trip to London. This meant
they had to leave their village, get on a bus to the nearest
town, and there catch the train for London. It was all a big
adventure for them, as they had never done anything like it
before. To eat on the journey, they had bought some
bananas. They'd never eaten bananas before either.
They got on the train and were marvelling at the speed. One
man decided to try his banana, but just as he was taking a
bite the train entered a tunnel.
'Have you eaten your banana yet?' he called out to his friend.
'No,' replied his friend.
'Well, don't' said the first man. 'I took one bite of mine and
went blind.'

Joke 2

A motorist driving through the country stopped for a

hitch-hiker who was holding the halter of a cow.

'I can give you a lift,' he said, 'but I can't take your cow.'

'Don't worry,' said the hitch-hiker, 'she'll follow us in her own time.'

So the hitch-hiker got in and the motorist started up. He

drove at thirty miles an hour and the cow trotted along

behind him. He drove at forty miles an hour and the cow was

still trotting along behind him. He drove at fifty miles an hour

yet the cow was somehow managing to keep pace with him.

But he noticed in his mirror that the cow seemed to be tiring,

as her tongue was hanging out of her mouth. 'I'm worried

about your cow,' said the motorist to his passenger, 'her

tongue is hanging out of her mouth to the right.'

'Oh, that's all right,' said the hitch-hiker, 'that means she's

going to overtake!'

23 JIGSAW READING 3

Mr Knott* was a teacher.

* pronounced 'not'

He taught in a big school in London.

He lived a long way from the school, so he was usually quite tired when he got home.

At 9 o'clock one evening, when he was in bed, the telephone bell rang in the hall of his small house.

So he went downstairs, picked up the telephone and said, 'This is Cardiff 316523, who's speaking, please?'

'Watt*,' a man answered.

* pronounced 'what'

'What's your name, please?' said Mr Knott.*

* pronounced 'not'

'Watt's* my name,' was the answer.

* pronounced 'what's'

'Yes, I asked you that. What's your name, please?' Mr Knott* said again.

* pronounced 'not'

'I told you. Watt's* my name,' said the other man.
'Are you Jack Smith?'

* pronounced 'what's'

'No, I'm not,' answered Mr Knott.*

* pronounced 'not'

'Will you give me your name, please?' said Mr Watt.*

* pronounced 'what'

'Will Knott,*' answered Mr Knott.

* pronounced 'not'

Both Mr Watt* and Mr Will Knott* put their telephones down angrily and thought, 'That was a rude, stupid man!'

* pronounced 'what' & 'not'

Game: What's my (uncle's) job?

Answer:

Yes,	always usually often sometimes	No,	never hardly ever not usually	I don't know I'm not sure

Ask:

Does he/she work	indoors? alone? in a shop? etc.
Does her/she use	a typewriter? his/her hands? etc.
Does he/she	need to drive? get dirty? meet people? make things? etc.

© Penguin Books 1995

Game: What do I like doing in my free time?

Answer:

Yes,	I do sometimes	No,	I don't not usually	I don't know I'm not sure

Ask:

Do you do this	indoors? alone? during the day? etc.	
Do you need	any equipment a ball etc.	to do this?
Do you use	your hands a mchine etc.	when you do this?
Do you	wear special clothing walk a lot etc.	when you do this?
Is it anything to do with	music? sport? cars etc.	

© Penguin Books 1995

Game: Which country am I thinking of?

Answer:

Yes,	it is they do there is/are a few/lots I think so	No,	it isn't they don't there isn't/aren't not much/many	I don't know I'm not sure

Ask:

Is this country	in Europe/Asia/etc? next to Sweden/Belgium/etc? large/small hot in the summer? etc.	
Do they	speak English/French/etc. drink tea/wine/etc. have a Queen/President/etc. etc.	in this country?
Is there	a good football team any oil a professional army etc.	in this country?
Are there any	mountains lakes car factories etc.	in this country?
Are there	many people lots of immigrants wild animals etc.	in this country?

Student A

Fill in this form about your partner.

Your partner:		Yes	No	Correct?
1	enjoys smoking.			
2	likes going to parties.			
3	doesn't often lose his/her temper.			
4	is romantic.			
5	thinks a woman's place is in the home.			
6	wants a big family.			
7	prefers pop music to classical music.			
8	can whistle loudly.			
9	has a dog.			
10	eats more fish than meat.			
11	has never tried windsurfing.			
12	isn't afraid of mice.			

When you have finished, check to see if you are correct by asking your partner questions. (Your partner will also ask you questions. Answer YES or NO.)

Student B

Fill in this form about your partner.

Your partner:		Yes	No	Correct?
1	enjoys going to discos.			
2	likes learning foreign languages.			
3	doesn't often go to the cinema.			
4	is not very good with money.			
5	thinks it is wrong to drink alcohol.			
6	wants to be very rich one day.			
7	prefers football to tennis.			
8	can cook well.			
9	has a cat.			
10	eats more pasta than meat.			
11	has never tried skating.			
12	isn't afraid of snakes.			

When you have finished, check to see if you are correct by asking your partner questions. (Your partner will also ask you questions. Answer YES or NO.)

28 THINGS WE WERE GOING TO DO

Student A

Imagine that you and your partner were at school together and that you meet at an airport several years later. When you were friends at school:

YOU TOLD HIM/HER YOU WERE GOING TO:	and YOUR PARTNER TOLD YOU HE/SHE WAS GOING TO:
leave home at 17 ✓ become a pop singer ✓ move to Los Angeles buy your parents a big house marry a foreigner ✓ have two children write a musical ✓ own a race horse grow your hair long ✓ have lots of money (✓ = *these came true*)	go to university become a doctor or a pilot buy a sports car marry Mark (or Emma) Taylor have lots of children move to London work abroad learn to fly an aeroplane write a novel make a lot of money

Find out what happened to his/her plans. He/she will also ask you about yours. Be prepared to use your imagination and try to ask lots of questions about why his/her plans came true or didn't come true.

Student B

Imagine that you and your partner were at school together and that you meet at an airport several years later. When you were friends at school:

YOU TOLD HIM/HER YOU WERE GOING TO:	and YOUR PARTNER TOLD YOU HE/SHE WAS GOING TO:
go to university ✓ become a doctor or a pilot buy a sports car ✓ marry Mark (or Emma) Taylor have lots of children move to London ✓ work abroad ✓ learn to fly an aeroplane write a novel make a lot of money ✓ (✓ = *these came true*)	leave home at 17 become a pop singer move to Los Angeles buy your parents a big house marry a foreigner have two children write a musical own a race horse grow your hair long have lots of money

Find out what happened to his/her plans. He/she will also ask you about yours. Be prepared to use your imagination and try to ask lots of questions about why his/her plans came true or didn't come true.

29 ASKING AND ANSWERING QUESTIONS ABOUT PHOTOGRAPHS

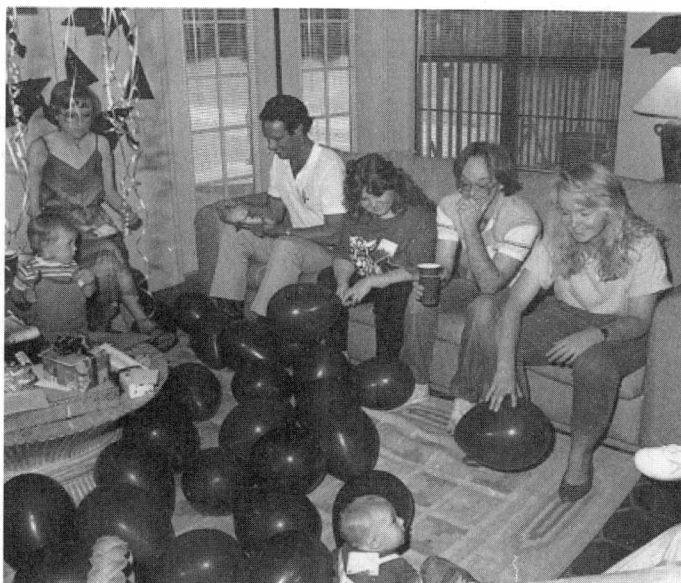

© Penguin Books 1995

Student A

Imagine you took the above photographs. Describe them to your partner, for example, what the occasion was, who the people were, etc. Your partner will probably ask you questions, so be prepared to use your imagination.

You can start by asking your partner:

Would you like to see some photographs?

Student B

Your partner is going to show you some photographs. Get him/her to talk about them as much as you can – especially about the people in them – by asking lots of questions, e.g. Who are these people? Who's this woman here on the right? What's this man's name? What's he doing? What's that building behind them? etc.

Student A

Imagine that one of the above photographs is of the first person you were ever really in love with. Your partner is a close friend of yours. You are going to tell him/her about this person. Before you start, think of the following:

- his/her name
- how old you were when you first met him/her and where you met
- how long you went out together
- what he/she was like
- what sort of things you used to do together
- if you hoped to marry him/her
- why you split up

Your partner will probably ask you lots of questions, so be prepared to use your imagination. You can start by saying:

Would you like to see a photo of the boy/girl I first fell in love with?

Student B

Your partner is a close friend of yours. He/she is going to show you a photograph of his/her first 'real' love. Find out as much as you can about this person by asking questions.

For example, try to find out:

- his/her name
- how your friend met him/her and where they met
- if it was love at first sight
- how long they went out together
- what sort of a person he/she was
- if your friend's parents liked him/her
- why they split up
- if your friend has seen him/her since
- if this person is now married

Try to think of at least fifteen questions to ask before you start.

31 ANSWERING AN ADVERTISEMENT

Student A

> THIRD PERSON
> required to share
> large house.
> Central. Phone
> 846592.

You have been sharing a large house with two other people for nearly two years. One of them has now decided to leave so you have to find someone to take his/her place. You have put the above advertisement in the local newspaper. Someone (your partner) phones you up about it.

Before you start, think about the following:

- where the house is situated
- when the person can move in
- how much the rent is
- how much of the house is shared
- who does the cleaning, etc.
- anything else you can think of (e.g. near the shops, station, modern, central heating, etc.)

If the person is interested, arrange a day and time when he/she can come and see the house.

© Penguin Books 1995

Student B

> THIRD PERSON
> required to share
> large house.
> Central. Phone
> 846592.

You have just moved to this town and are looking for a house or flat to rent. You see the above advertisement and decided to phone up about it. Your partner answers the phone.

Before you start, think of some questions to ask. For example, you might want to know:

- where it is
- when you can move in
- how much the rent is
- what the other people are like
- how much of the house is shared
- if everyone helps with the cleaning, cooking, etc.
- what 'your room' is like
- if it is near a supermarket, etc.

If you are interested, try to arrange a day and time to go and see it. You can start by saying:

Good (morning). I'm phoning about your advertisement in the paper.

© Penguin Books 1995

You went to a party last Tuesday. It was your cousin's birthday. She was 18.   1

Someone else in the group:

1 went to Brighton last Wednesday.
   Find out who he/she went to see.

2 saw the film *Tarzan meets James Bond* last week.
   Find out when he/she went to see it.

3 bought a second-hand car for £4,000 last week.
   Find out what sort of car he/she bought.

You bought a car last Sunday – a white second-hand Volvo. You paid £4,000 for it.   2

Someone else in the group:

1 went to the cinema last weekend.
   Find out what he/she thought of the film.

2 went to his/her uncle's birthday party last week.
   Find out which day that was.

3 went to Brighton last Wednesday.
   Find out how he/she got there.

You went to the cinema last Saturday. You saw the film *Tarzan meets James Bond*. It was a very good film.   3

Someone else in the group:

1 went to a party last Tuesday.
   Find out whose party it was.

2 went to Brighton by car last week.
   Find out when he/she went there.

3 bought a red car last week.
   Find out what sort of car he/she bought.

You went to Brighton last Wednesday to see your grandmother. You went there by train.   4

Someone else in the group:

1 bought a Volvo last weekend.
   Find out if it was new or second-hand.

2 went to his/her cousin's birthday party last week.
   Find out on which day it was.

3 saw a terrible film at the cinema last week.
   Find out what it was called.

You went to a party last Saturday. It was your uncle's birthday. He was 50. **5**

Someone else in the group:

1 bought a car last Sunday.
   Find out how much he/she paid for it.

2 saw the film *The Last Cowboy* last week.
   Find out when he/she went to see it.

3 went to Brighton last Thursday.
   Find out how he/she got there.

You bought a car last Saturday – a brand-new Ford. It was red. **6**

Someone else in the group:

1 went to a party last Saturday.
   Find out whose party it was.

2 went to Brighton last week.
   Find out when he/she went there.

3 saw a good film at the cinema last week.
   Find out what the film was called.

You went to the cinema last Tuesday. You saw the film *The Last Cowboy*. It was terrible. **7**

Someone else in the group:

1 went to Brighton last Thursday.
   Find out who he/she went to see.

2 bought a Ford car last week.
   Find out on which day he/she bought it.

3 went to his/her cousin's birthday party last week.
   Find out how old the cousin was.

You went to Brighton last Thursday to see some friends. You went there by car. **8**

Someone else in the group:

1 went to the cinema last Tuesday.
   Find out what he/she thought of the film.

2 bought a new car last weekend.
   Find out what colour it was.

3 went to his/her uncle's birthday party last week.
   Find out how old the uncle was.

33 GETTING TO KNOW YOU 1

Take it in turns to interview your partner and to write down his/her answers on the following form.

First names: _____ Surname: _____

Place of birth: _____

Nationality: _____

Present address: _____

_____

How long at above address: _____

Other towns lived in: _____

Married: Yes/No

Present job: _____

OR

School/College/University: _____

Interests/Hobbies: _____

Reason for learning English: _____

Started learning English in: _____

Other foreign languages spoken: _____

Favourite food: _____

Pet hates: _____

Greatest hero: _____

Greatest invention: _____

Last foreign country visited: _____

(My) good points: _____

(My) bad points: _____

Main ambition: _____

When you have both finished, find another partner. Now take it in turns to tell each other about the person you interviewed.

Student A

*Read through the following sentences, then write down your answers on **a separate piece of paper**. Number your answers 1–12.*

Write down:

1 the first name of the person who influenced you most when you were a child.
2 the name of the town or village where you were born.
3 the name of the subject you hated most at school.
4 your favourite possession (e.g. a car, a watch, a computer, etc.)
5 the name of the job you would like to have if you could choose any job in the world.
6 the surname of someone *(still alive)* you don't like very much.

7 two things you really enjoy doing.
8 the year when you first went abroad. If you have never been abroad, the year you first went away on holiday.
9 the name of the most beautiful area in your country.
10 the year in which something really important happened to you.
11 the number of years you have had your present job. If you are unemployed, how long you have been out of work. If you are still studying, write down the year you think you will start work.
12 two things that worry you.

*When you have finished, work with your partner. Don't let him/her see this paper. Instead, give him/her your paper with the answers on and take it in turns to ask and answer questions about the things you have written. For example, **What does this date mean**?*

Try to make your partner talk as much as possible.

Student B

*Read through the following sentences, then write down your answers **on a separate piece of paper**. Number your answers 1–12.*

Write down:

1 the number of years you have lived in your present town or village.
2 the first name of someone you really disliked at school.
3 the name of the town or country where you had the nicest holiday you can remember.
4 two things you hate doing (e.g. ironing, homework, etc.)
5 the name of the subject you were worst at when you were at school.
6 the surname of your favourite relative.
7 what your present job is. If you are unemployed, what your last job was. If you are still studying, the job you hope to get.

8 the number of people there are in your family. Include parents, grandparents, brothers, sisters, own children.
9 a date where something really important happened to you.
10 anything you are afraid of (e.g. spiders, death, etc.)
11 the name of the country you would like to go to if you ever decided to emigrate.
12 the full name of the person *(living or dead)* you admire most.

*When you have finished, work with your partner. Don't let him/her see this paper. Instead, give him/her your paper with the answers on and take it in turns to ask and answer questions about the things you have written. For example, **What does this year mean**?*

Try to make your partner talk as much as possible.

tennis	by boat	frightened	tomorrow
Stockholm	Spain	blue	yesterday
Margaret Thatcher	a cow	strawberries	Beethoven
a cat	vegetables	on Sunday	in June
I love you	Bad luck!	thirsty	How do you do
milk	in 1990	last year	my father
No, thank you	Yes, I can	No, never	a computer
2 weeks ago	bananas	a Fancy Dress party	the theatre
Shakespeare	nervous	angry	a newspaper
on holiday	Keep the change!	John Lennon	for sale

I'm never going to speak to (him/her) again!	I'm moving next week.	I saw (him/her) again this morning.
I'm in love!	I don't know what to do about it.	That's the last time I ever do that!
I wish they would move!	I wish I hadn't told (him/her) now!	I had a really great time last night.
I've decided to quit my job.	I'm ever so worried!	I can't stand my new (boss/ teacher)!

37 WHAT ARE THE MISSING NUMBERS?

Student A

Find the missing numbers.

	A	B	C	D	E	F
1		107		23	172	
2	72		58			1,017
3		156		34		328
4		527	95			66

Take it in turns to ask and answer, e.g. **What's the number in square C1? It's...**

When you have finished, compare your squares.

Student B

Find the missing numbers.

	A	B	C	D	E	F
1	43		828			89
2		444		950	118	
3	1,253		608		0	
4	268			739	217	

Take it in turns to ask and answer, e.g. **What's the number in square F4? It's...**

When you have finished, compare your squares.

38   WHAT ARE THE MISSING DATES?

Student A

Find the missing dates.

	A	B	C	D	E	F
1	3rd	9th		18th	30th	
2		4th			2nd	
3	15th		11th		24th	
4	1st		22nd			19th

Take it in turns to ask and answer, e.g. **What's the date in square C1?**   **It's the…**

When you have finished, compare your squares.

Student B

Find the missing dates.

	A	B	C	D	E	F
1			23rd			13th
2	21st		27th	20th		6th
3		8th		5th		16th
4		10th		7th	12th	

Take it in turns to ask and answer, e.g. **What's the date in square A4?**   **It's the…**

When you have finished, compare your squares.

39 FOUR PEOPLE

Student A

Work with a partner. Ask and answer questions to fill in the missing information about the following four people.

Name	**Philippa**	**Kurt**	**Maria**	**Jack**
Date of birth		1 June 1944		31 April 1975
Country of origin			Portugal	New Zealand
Married or single	single		married	
Number of children	none		2 boys, 1 girl	
Home town		Berlin		Wellington
Present job	actress			policeman
Interests or hobbies	music	gardening	horse riding	playing rugby
Dislikes		cold weather	doing the washing-up	
		people who snore	writing letters	
Main ambition	to win an Oscar			to visit Europe

Before you start, work out what questions to ask, e.g.

> What is Philippa's date of birth?
> What is Kurt's present job?
> Where does Maria live?
> What two things does Jack dislike?
> etc.

When you have finished, compare your tables.

39 FOUR PEOPLE

Student B

Work with a partner. Ask and answer questions to fill in the missing information about the following four people.

Name	Philippa	Kurt	Maria	Jack
Date of birth	18 February 1970		12 August 1958	
Country of origin	Wales	Germany		
Married or single		married		married
Number of children		1 boy		2 girls
Home town	Swansea		Oporto	
Present job		journalist	teacher	
Interests or hobbies	learning languages	painting	playing tennis	playing golf
Dislikes	ironing			people who smoke
	getting up early			going to the dentist
Main ambition		to write a novel	to travel to America	

Before you start, work out what questions to ask, e.g.

Is Philippa married or single?
What is one of Kurt's interests or hobbies?
What two things does Maria dislike?
What is Jack's job?
etc.

When you have finished, compare your tables.

Student A

Work with a partner. Ask and answer questions to find the missing information in the following table.

At...	She usually:	At...	She usually...
(clock)	wakes up	(clock)	gets home
(clock)	has a shower	(clock)	takes her dog for a walk
(clock)		(clock)	has a cup of tea and reads the newspaper
(clock)	has breakfast – usually _____	(clock)	has dinner
(clock)	drives to work	(clock)	telephones her _____
(clock)		(clock)	watches the News on television
(clock)	has lunch – usually at an Italian restaurant	(clock)	goes to bed
(clock)	starts work again	(clock)	reads for a while
(clock)	finishes work	(clock)	falls asleep

Before you start, work out which questions to ask, e.g.

What time does Jane (have a shower)?
When does she (start work again)?
What does she do (at a quarter to eight in the morning?)
etc.

When you have finished, compare your tables.

Student B

Work with a partner. Ask and answer questions to find the missing information in the following table.

At...	She usually:	At...	She usually...
(clock)	wakes up	(clock)	gets home
(clock)	has a shower	(clock)	
(clock)	gets dressed	(clock)	has a cup of tea and reads the newspaper
(clock)	has breakfast – usually tea and toast	(clock)	
(clock)		(clock)	telephones her father
(clock)	starts work	(clock)	watches _____ on television
(clock)	has lunch – usually at _____	(clock)	goes to bed
(clock)	starts work again	(clock)	
(clock)	finishes work	(clock)	falls asleep

Before you start, work out which questions to ask, e.g.

What time does Jane (wake up)?
When does she (finish work)?
What does she do (at a quarter past seven in the evening?)
etc.

When you have finished, compare your tables.

Student A

Work with a partner. Ask and answer questions to find the missing information in the following short biographies of Picasso and David Livingstone.

WHO WAS PICASSO?

Picasso was born in 18_____ in _____, Spain. When he started work, the great painters of the Impressionist movement were still alive. His early pictures – done mainly in blue – showed the _____ he saw around him in Barcelona.

Later he moved to Paris where he worked with Georges _____ on pictures showing figures as fragments of geometric shapes – the style we know as _____.

He became more deeply involved with politics, especially during the Spanish Civil War. One of Picasso's most famous paintings is *Guernica*, which depicts _____. Picasso died in the south of France in 1973.

WHO WAS DAVID LIVINGSTONE?

David Livingstone was born in 1813. He went to Africa in 1841, to _____ and to teach Christianity to the Africans.

Livingstone made several journeys on foot into _____. He saw the Kalahari Desert and followed the River Zambezi to discover the magnificent _____. He was horrified by _____ and did all he could to stop it.

In 1866 Livingstone set off to search for the source of the River Nile. Nothing was heard of him until in _____ an expedition led by _____ found him near Lake Tanganyika. Though ill, Livingstone went on exploring until he died, in _____. Two Africans carried his body over 2,000 kilometres to the coast, and returned it to Britain.

Before you start, work out which questions to ask, e.g.

When was Picasso born?
What did he see around him in Barcelona?
Why did David Livingstone go to Africa?
etc.

When you have finished, compare your biographies.

© Penguin Books 1995

Student B

Work with a partner. Ask and answer questions to find the missing information in the following short biographies of Picasso and David Livingstone.

WHO WAS PICASSO?

Picasso was born in 1881 in Malaga, Spain. When he started work, the great painters of the _____ movement were still alive. His early pictures – done mainly in _____ – showed the poverty he saw around him in Barcelona.

Later he moved to _____ where he worked with Georges Braque on pictures showing figures as fragments of geometric shapes – the style we know as cubism.

He became more deeply involved with _____, especially during the _____ War. One of Picasso's most famous paintings is *Guernica*, which depicts the destruction of a Spanish town. Picasso died in _____ in 1973.

WHO WAS DAVID LIVINGSTONE?

David Livingstone was born in _____. He went to _____ in 1841, to practise medicine and to teach Christianity to the Africans.

Livingstone made several journeys on foot into the unknown heart of Africa. He saw the Kalahari Desert and followed the River _____ to discover the magnificent Victoria Falls. He was horrified by the slave trade and did all he could to stop it.

In 1866 Livingstone set off to search for _____. Nothing was heard of him until in 1871 an expedition led by Henry Morton Stanley found him near _____. Though ill, Livingstone went on exploring until he died, in 1873. Two Africans carried his body _____ kilometres to the coast, and returned it to Britain.

Before you start, work out which questions to ask, e.g.

The painters of which movement were still alive when Picasso started painting?
Where did he move to?
When was David Livingstone born?
etc.

When you have finished, compare your biographies.

Student A

Work with a partner. Ask and answer questions to find the missing information in the following extracts from a book of amazing facts.

Strange but true

1 Elephants cannot jump.
2 Queen Elizabeth I of England _____ at an early age.
3 Until 1957 it was illegal to _____ in Wales on a Sunday.
4 _____ were first developed to help the blind.
5 For the first six or seven months of our lives, we can do something that we are never able to do again; swallow and breathe at the same time.
6 In order to be the last name in the local telephone directory, a Chicago man changed his name to Zeke Zzzypt.
7 Sir Winston Churchill was a well-known Shakespearean actor before he became a politician.
8 The yo-yo was originally a Filipino jungle weapon.
9 Goldfish will often turn white if _____.
10 When Ian Fleming wrote his first James Bond book, his 007 hero was called _____.
11 King Louis XIV of France was the first person, male or female, to wear high heels.
12 The Germans used to keep frogs as live barometers because they _____.
13 Indian ink actually comes from _____.
14 To conserve metal, the _____ during World War II were made of wood.
15 The word 'tip' is an abbreviation of '_____'.
16 _____ was first invented by the Chinese nearly 2,000 years ago.
17 It is impossible to sneeze and keep your eyes open at the same time.
18 Bumping foreheads with a handshake is the traditional greeting in Tibet.
19 The corkscrew was first invented to pull out teeth.
20 When George I came to the throne of England he could not speak a word of English.

Before you start, work out which questions to ask, e.g.

What happened to Queen Elizabeth of England at an early age?
Where does Indian ink actually come from?
Why did the Germans used to keep frogs as live barometers?
etc.

When you have finished, compare your answers and also try to work out which of the above facts are completely untrue. (There are 5 altogether.)

42   IT'S A FACT!

Student B

Work with a partner. Ask and answer questions to find the missing information in the following extracts from a book of amazing facts.

Strange but true

1 Elephants cannot _____.
2 Queen Elizabeth I of England went completely bald at an early age.
3 Until 1957 it was illegal to go swimming in Wales on a Sunday.
4 Typewriters were first developed to help the blind.
5 For the first six or seven months of our lives, we can do something that we are never able to do again; _____.
6 In order to be the last name in the local telephone directory, a Chicago man changed his name to _____.
7 Sir Winston Churchill was a _____ before he became a politician.
8 The yo-yo was originally a _____.
9 Goldfish will often turn white if left in a darkened room.
10 When Ian Fleming wrote his first James Bond book, his 007 hero was called Rupert de Vere.
11 King Louis XIV of France was the first person, male or female, to wear _____.
12 The Germans used to keep frogs as live barometers because they croak when the pressure drops.
13 Indian ink actually comes from China.
14 To conserve metal, the Oscars given out in the Academy Awards during World War II were made of wood.
15 The word 'tip' is an abbreviation of 'To Insure Promptness'.
16 A form of golf was first invented by the Chinese nearly 2,000 years ago.
17 It is impossible to _____ at the same time.
18 Bumping foreheads with a handshake is the traditional greeting in _____.
19 The corkscrew was first invented to _____.
20 When George I came to the throne of England he could not _____.

Before you start, work out which questions to ask, e.g.

What was the yo-yo originally?
What can't elephants do?
Where/In which country is bumping foreheads with a handshake the traditional greeting?
etc.

When you have finished, compare your answers and also try to work out which of the above facts are completely untrue. (There are 5 altogether.)

43 HOLIDAY PLANS

Student A

Work with a partner. Ask and answer questions to find the missing information in the following tables.

Name:	Peter Brown
Destination:	
Travel plans:	
Date of departure:	14 July
Length of stay:	3 weeks
Plans while on holiday:	

Name:	Amanda Smith
Destination:	Australia
Travel plans:	
Date of departure:	
Length of stay:	6 weeks
Plans while on holiday:	visit Alice Springs
	see a kangaroo
	go surfing

Name:	Kevin Blake
Destination:	India
Travel plans:	by air
Date of departure:	
Length of stay:	
Plans while on holiday:	see the Taj Mahal
	eat a real curry
	visit Calcutta

Name:	Anne Harris
Destination:	
Travel plans:	by car
Date of departure:	21 June
Length of stay:	
Plans while on holiday:	

Before you start, work out which questions to ask, e.g.

Where is Peter Brown going for his holiday?
How is he travelling?
What is Anne Harris planning to do on holiday?
etc.

When you have finished, compare your tables. You can also discuss your own holiday plans.

43 HOLIDAY PLANS

Student B

Work with a partner. Ask and answer questions to find the missing information in the following tables.

Name:	Peter Brown
Destination:	Sweden
Travel plans:	by boat
Date of departure:	
Length of stay:	
Plans while on holiday:	visit Stockholm
	see an elk
	meet a nice Swedish girl

Name:	Amanda Smith
Destination:	
Travel plans:	by air
Date of departure:	22 August
Length of stay:	
Plans while on holiday:	

Name:	Kevin Blake
Destination:	
Travel plans:	
Date of departure:	1 September
Length of stay:	1 month
Plans while on holiday:	

Name:	Anne Harris
Destination:	Scotland
Travel plans:	
Date of departure:	
Length of stay:	2 weeks
Plans while on holiday:	climb Ben Nevis
	look for the Loch Ness monster
	visit Edinburgh

Before you start, work out which questions to ask, e.g.

Where is Amanda Smith going on holiday?
How long is she going to stay there?
What is Kevin Blake planning to do on holiday?
etc.

When you have finished, compare your tables. You can also discuss your own holiday plans.

44   A FAMILY TREE

Work in a group of six. Each of you has some information about the James family. Working together, fill in the missing names in the family tree and also the jobs of the people in the middle row.

(You are only allowed to read out – not show – the pieces of information you have.)

The James Family Tree

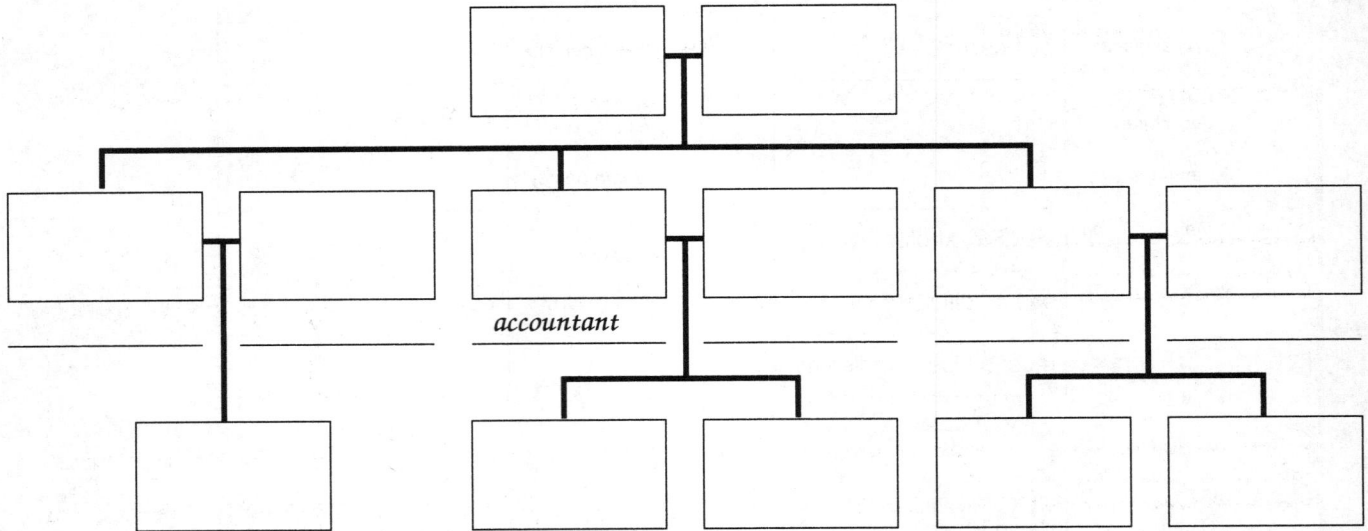

accountant

© Penguin Books 1995

1   Tom's grandfather is called Douglas.
2   Sally's husband is an electrician.
3   Anne has two boys.
4   Rebecca is Amanda's cousin.

1   Amanda's mother is a nurse.
2   Peter has two daughters.
3   Sylvia's daughter-in-law is a doctor.
4   David and Peter are brothers.

1   The editor is married to David.
2   Mark is Amanda's father.
3   Joanna and Rebecca are sisters.
4   Douglas has two sons and a daughter.

1   Sally is Bob's aunt.
2   One of Peter's nephews is called Bob.
3   David married Anne.
4   Amanda is an only child.

1   Joanna's father is a teacher.
2   Sylvia is a grandmother.
3   Nina is Peter's wife.
4   Mark is Sylvia's son-in-law.

1   Peter is Sylvia's son.
2   Sally has two brothers.
3   The accountant is called David.
4   Bob and Tom are brothers.

45 MRS GREEN'S FRUIT & VEGETABLE STALL

Work in groups of four. Mrs Green is very fussy about how she lays out her display of fruit and vegetables. Each of you has some information about where she puts the various things. Working together, fill in the names of the fruit and vegetables according to where they are on her stall. When you have finished, you should be able to work out where she has put the carrots.

(You are only allowed to read out – not show – the pieces of information you have.)

Where are the carrots?

Left   *Right*

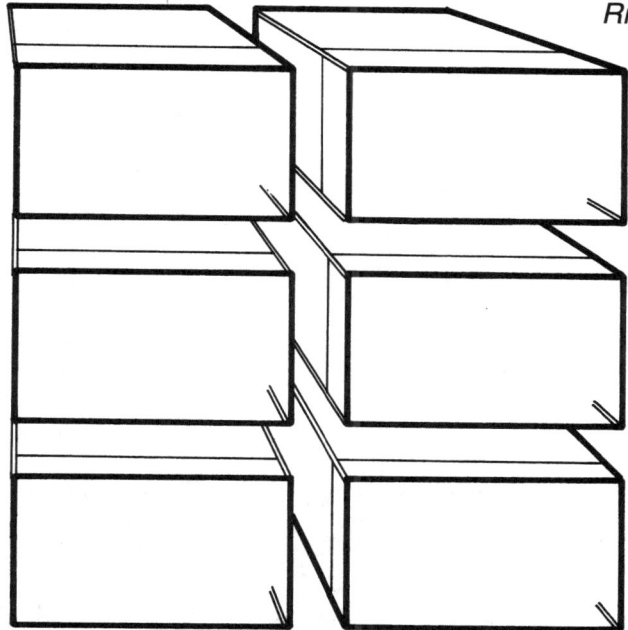

| apples | carrots | grapes | oranges | pineapples | potatoes |
| cabbage | cucumbers | lettuce | peaches | plums | sprouts |

© Penguin Books 1995

---

1 No two fruits or vegetables are directly next to each other.
2 The cucumbers are on the left of the grapes.
3 The potatoes are in the bottom right corner.

1 No two fruits or vegetables are directly above or below each other.
2 The cucumbers are in the bottom row.
3 The plums are in the same column as the peaches.

---

1 The plums are above the cabbage.
2 The apples are between the lettuce and the sprouts.
3 The potatoes are in the same column as the sprouts.

1 The oranges are above the cucumbers.
2 The sprouts are above the pineapples.
3 The cucumbers are on the right of the peaches.

Work in groups A and B. You are A.

The crossword below is only half filled in. Group B also have a crossword that is only half filled in. Take it in turns to ask what the missing verbs are.

You can ask, for example, **'What's 7 across?'.**

When you answer, answer like this: **'It's the past tense of (bring).'**

Here are the verbs that Group B will ask for. Before you start, make sure you know the infinitive (eat, bite, etc.) for each of them.

ate	drank	kept	said	taught
bit	dug	lit	sat	threw
broke	fell	lost	shook	told
brought	forgot	rode	spoke	understood
chose	fought			

46 HALF A CROSSWORD: IRREGULAR VERBS   Group B

Work in groups A and B. You are B.

The crossword below is only half filled in. Group A also have a crossword that is only half filled in. Take it in turns to ask what the missing verbs are.

You can ask, for example, **'What's 3 across?'.**

When you answer, answer like this: **'It's the past tense of (begin).'**

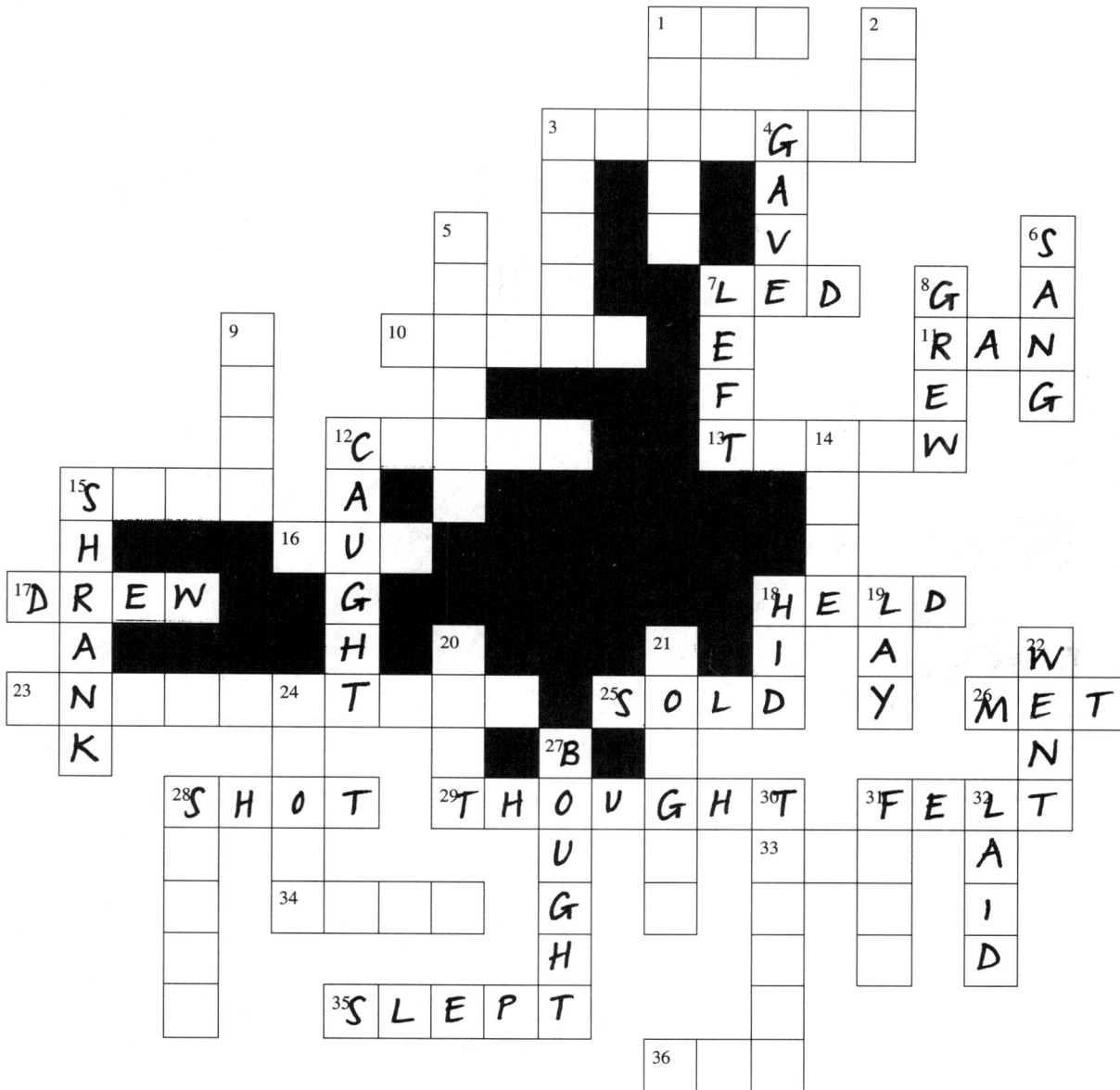

Here are the verbs that Group B will ask for. Before you start, make sure you know the infinitive (eat, bite, etc.) for each of them.

began	gave	lay	ran	slept
bought	grew	led	sang	sold
caught	held	left	shot	thought
drew	hid	met	shrank	went
felt	laid			

© Penguin Books 1995

47 FIND THE DIFFERENCES 1

Student A

Work with a partner. You both have a drawing of a block of flats where you can see people doing different things. But your drawings are not the same. There are 8 differences.

Ask and answer questions to try to find what is different. You can ask, e.g.

> **What's the (man, boy, woman, girl, people, etc.) doing in flat (20)?**
> **Is the (man, woman, dog, children, etc.) in flat (20) (reading a newspaper)?**
> etc.

When you have finished, compare your drawings.

Student B

Work with a partner. You both have a drawing of a block of flats where you can see people doing different things. But your drawings are not the same. There are 8 differences.

Ask and answer questions to try to find what is different. You can ask, e.g.

What's the *(man, boy, woman, girl, people, etc.)* **doing in flat** *(20)*?
Is the *(man, woman, dog, children, etc.)* **in flat** *(20)* *(doing the washing-up)*?
etc.

When you have finished, compare your drawings.

© Penguin Books 1995

Student A

Work with a partner. You both have an account of Andrew Scott's life history. But your accounts are not the same. There are 12 differences.

Take it in turns to ask and answer questions to try to find what is different. Put a circle around any differences you find. (But you needn't tell your partner!)

You can ask, e.g.

Was Andrew Scott born on 9th June, 1955?	*or*	**When was Andrew Scott born?**
Did he start work at a post office in August, 1972?	*or*	**When did he start work at a post office?**
Was Julie Parker an actress?	*or*	**What did Julie Parker do?**
etc.		

(NOTE: Only answer the questions your partner asks. Do not give him/her any extra information.)

The Life History of Andrew Scott

Andrew Scott was born in Brighton on 9th June, 1955. His father was a policeman and his mother was a tax inspector. He started school when he was five and left school when he was sixteen. In August 1972 he started work at a post office in the centre of Brighton. He stayed there for five years. Then in September 1978 he moved to London. He got a new job at a travel agency not far from Buckingham Palace.

Six months later he met Julie Parker at a party. They fell in love and got married on 26th April, 1979. Julie was an actress and when she got the chance to work in America, Andrew gave up his job and went with her. They stayed in America for eleven years altogether. During this time, Julie made ten films and was the star of a television series called *Two People*.

Andrew started writing books and in June 1982 his first book, *Brighton Sand*, was published. It sold nearly a million copies. A year later, their first child was born. They called him David after Andrew's grandfather. They had two more children while they were in America – Emily, who was born in 1985 and Simon who was born in 1987.

In March 1991 they moved back to Britain. They lived in Leeds at first, then three years ago they bought a very big house near Brighton. This is where they now live.

When you have finished, compare your texts.

Student B

Work with a partner. You both have an account of Andrew Scott's life history. But your accounts are not the same. There are 12 differences.

Take it in turns to ask and answer questions to try to find what is different. Put a circle around any differences you find. (But you needn't tell your partner!)

You can ask, e.g.

Was Andrew Scott born on 19th July, 1955? *or*   **When was Andrew Scott born?**
Did he start work at a bank in August, 1972?   *or*   **When did he start work at a bank?**
Was Julie Parker an actress?   *or*   **What did Julie Parker do?**
etc.

(NOTE: Only answer the questions your partner asks. Do not give him/her any extra information.)

The Life History of Andrew Scott

Andrew Scott was born in Brighton on 19th July, 1955. His father was a policeman and his mother was an estate agent. He started school when he was five and left school when he was sixteen. In August 1972 he started work at a bank in the centre of Brighton. He stayed there for five years. Then in September 1978 he moved to London. He got a new job at a travel agency not far from Trafalgar Square.

Six months later he met Julie Parker while he was on holiday. They fell in love and got married on 26th April, 1980. Julie was an actress and when she got the chance to work in America, Andrew gave up his job and went with her. They stayed in America for eleven years altogether. During this time, Julie made ten films and was the star of a television series called *Chicago*.

Andrew started writing books and in June 1982 his second book, *Brighton Sand*, was published. It sold over a million copies. A year later, their first child was born. They called him David after Andrew's father. They had two more children while they were in America – Emily, who was born in 1985 and Simon who was born in 1987.

In March 1991 they moved back to Britain. They lived in York at first, then two years ago they bought a very big house near Brighton. This is where they now live.

When you have finished, compare your texts.

Student A

Work with a partner. You both have a copy of four people's diaries. But some of the things marked in them are not the same. There are 11 differences altogether.

Take it in turns to ask and answer questions to try to find which things are different. Put a circle around any differences you find. (But you needn't tell your partner!)

You can ask, e.g.

Where is Peter going on Wednesday?
Is Colin having his eyes tested on Monday?
At what time on Sunday is Emma visiting her grandparents?
etc.

(NOTE: Only answer the questions your partner asks. Do not give him/her any extra information.)

Peter's diary

22 Monday play squash 7 o'clock	Friday 26 spend evening with Cathy
23 Tuesday	Saturday 27 play football 2.15 meet Cathy 7.30
24 Wednesday go to the dentist 10.30	Sunday 28
25 Thursday visit Aunty Jane 6.30	

Helen's diary

22 Monday go to pottery classes 7.15	Friday 26 meet friends at disco 9 o'clock
23 Tuesday stay in and wash hair	Saturday 27 drive to Watford to see Paul (after 6)
24 Wednesday	Sunday 28
25 Thursday take cat to the vet 10.30	

Emma's diary

22 Monday go for a meal with Sally 7.30	Friday 26
23 Tuesday take car to the garage 11.30	Saturday 27 go swimming 10.30 meet Sally and Jenny 8.15
24 Wednesday have lunch with Nick 1.30	Sunday 28 visit grandma and grandpa 4.30
25 Thursday	

Colin's diary

22 Monday have eyes tested 11 o'clock	Friday 26 stay in and tidy the flat
23 Tuesday	Saturday 27 meet dad for lunch 12.30 have party at flat
24 Wednesday go to the cinema with Steve and Michael 7.15	Sunday 28 phone mum and dad 10 30 watch TV 7.30
25 Thursday	

When you have finished, compare your diaries.

Student B

Work with a partner. You both have a copy of four people's diaries. But some of the things marked in them are not the same. There are 11 differences altogether.

Take it in turns to ask and answer questions to try to find which things are different. Put a circle around any differences you find. (But you needn't tell your partner!)

You can ask, e.g.

Where is Peter going on Friday?
Is Helen taking the dog to the vet on Thursday?
At what time on Sunday is Colin phoning his parents?
etc.

(NOTE: Only answer the questions your partner asks. Do not give him/her any extra information.)

Peter's diary	
22 Monday play squash 7 o'clock	Friday 26 go to cinema with Cathy
23 Tuesday go to the dentist 10.30	Saturday 27 play football 2.15 meet Cathy 8.30
24 Wednesday	Sunday 28
25 Thursday visit Aunty Jane 6.30	

Helen's diary	
22 Monday go to pottery classes 7.30	Friday 26 meet friends at disco 9 o'clock
23 Tuesday stay in and wash hair	Saturday 27 drive to Swindon to see Paul (after 6)
24 Wednesday	Sunday 28
25 Thursday take dog to the vet 10.30	

Emma's diary	
22 Monday go for a meal with Sally 7.30	Friday 26
23 Tuesday take mum to the doctor 11.30	Saturday 27 go swimming 10.30 meet Sally and Jenny 8.15
24 Wednesday	Sunday 28 visit grandma and grandpa 4.30
25 Thursday have lunch with Nick 1.30	

Colin's diary	
22 Monday have eyes tested 11 o'clock	Friday 26 stay in and tidy the flat
23 Tuesday	Saturday 27 meet dad for lunch 12.30 have party at flat
24 Wednesday go to the theatre with Steve and Michael 7.15	Sunday 28 phone mum and dad 10 30
25 Thursday	

When you have finished, compare your diaries.

50 FIND THE DIFFERENCES 4

Student A

Work with a partner. You both have a drawing of some people in a living room. But your drawings are not the same. There are at least 10 differences.

Ask and answer questions to try to find what is different. Put a circle around any differences you find. You can ask, e.g.

How many people are there in the room?
Are there any paintings on the wall?
Is the (man, woman, dog, etc.) reading a newspaper?
etc.

(NOTE: Only answer the questions your partner asks. Do not give him/her any extra information.)

When you have finished, compare your drawings.

50 FIND THE DIFFERENCES 4

Student B

Work with a partner. You both have a drawing of some people in a living room. But your drawings are not the same. There are at least 10 differences.

Ask and answer questions to try to find what is different. Put a circle around any differences you find. You can ask, e.g.

How many people are there in the room?
Are there any paintings on the wall?
Is the (man, woman, dog, etc.) reading a newspaper?
etc.

(NOTE: Only answer the questions your partner asks. Do not give him/her any extra information.)

When you have finished, compare your drawings.

51 HABITS QUESTIONNAIRE

Student A

Work with a partner. Take it in turns to ask each other questions and to write down your partner's answers.

Do you:	Yes, always	Yes, usually	Yes, often	Yes, sometimes	No, not usually	No, not very often	No, hardly ever	No never
get bored when you are alone?								
go abroad for your holidays?								
tidy up before visitors arrive?								
watch TV in the evening?								
go skiing in the winter?								
have a boiled egg for breakfast?								
feel nervous when you fly?								
go to bed early?								
get up before 7 o'clock?								
go out at weekends?								
remember your dreams?								
plan for the future?								

When you have finished, write down six things about your partner, e.g.

(Peter) usually goes abroad for his holidays.
He never goes to bed early.
etc.

Now find a new partner. Take it in turns to talk about the person you interviewed.

51 HABITS QUESTIONNAIRE

Student B

Work with a partner. Take it in turns to ask each other questions and to write down your partner's answers.

Do you:	Yes, always	Yes, usually	Yes, often	Yes, sometimes	No, not usually	No, not very often	No, hardly ever	No, never
wake up without an alarm clock?								
feel nervous when you meet new people?								
have lunch at home?								
listen to the news before you go to work/school?								
borrow books from the library?								
go shopping for food more than twice a week?								
drink tea or coffee in the evening?								
go to bed late?								
remember people's telephone numbers?								
go jogging?								
sing in the bath or shower?								
drive to work/school?								

When you have finished, write down six things about your partner, e.g.

(Maria) usually wakes up without an alarm clock.
She never goes to bed late.
etc.

Now find a new partner. Take it in turns to talk about the person you interviewed.

52 GROUP INTERVIEWS

Interview six other people in the class about **work** and write down their answers. (People may also ask you questions.)

Do you:	1	2	3	4	5	6
go to work by bus?						
work overtime?						
travel a lot in your job?						
work in the evenings?						
use a computer?						

Answer Key

1 = Yes, always   2 = Yes, usually   3 = Yes, sometimes
4 = No, not usually   5 = No, hardly ever   6 = No, never

1

Interview six other people in the class about **free time and entertainment** and write down their answers. (People may also ask you questions.)

Do you:	1	2	3	4	5	6
go out in the evenings?						
have many parties at home?						
go to the cinema?						
go dancing?						
spend the weekend with friends?						

Answer Key

1 = Yes, always   2 = Yes, usually   3 = Yes, sometimes
4 = No, not usually   5 = No, hardly ever   6 = No, never

2

Interview six other people in the class about **travel and holidays** and write down their answers. (People may also ask you questions.)

Do you:	1	2	3	4	5	6
use public transport?						
travel more than 5 kilometres a day?						
sunbathe a lot on holiday?						
have a skiing holiday in the winter?						
spend your summer holidays in your own country?						

Answer Key

1 = Yes, always   2 = Yes, usually   3 = Yes, sometimes
4 = No, not usually   5 = No, hardly ever   6 = No, never

3

52 GROUP INTERVIEWS (continued)

Interview six other people in the class about **relationships with other people** and write down their answers. (People may also ask you questions.)

Do you:	1	2	3	4	5	6
see one or more of your relatives at least once a week?						
like going to parties where you hardly know anyone?						
find it easy to talk to strangers?						
discuss your problems with a friend?						
find it hard to make new friends?						

Answer Key

1 = Yes, always   2 = Yes, usually   3 = Yes, sometimes
4 = No, not usually   5 = No, hardly ever   6 = No, never

4

Interview six other people in the class about **health** and write down their answers. (People may also ask you questions.)

Do you:	1	2	3	4	5	6
smoke more than 10 cigarettes a day?						
do some form of physical exercise at least once a week?						
sleep at least seven hours every night?						
catch a cold in the winter?						
eat lots of fruit and vegetables?						

Answer Key

1 = Yes, always   2 = Yes, usually   3 = Yes, sometimes
4 = No, not usually   5 = No, hardly ever   6 = No, never

5

Interview six other people in the class about **shopping** and write down their answers. (People may also ask you questions.)

Do you:	1	2	3	4	5	6
buy your food at the supermarket?						
go shopping for food more than twice a week?						
buy clothes more than once a month?						
wait for the sales before you buy clothes?						
enjoy shopping?						

Answer Key

1 = Yes, always   2 = Yes, usually   3 = Yes, sometimes
4 = No, not usually   5 = No, hardly ever   6 = No, never

6

52 GROUP INTERVIEWS (continued)

Interview six other people in the class about **food and drink** and write down their answers. (People may also ask you questions.)

Do you:	1	2	3	4	5	6
have three meals a day?						
go to a restaurant for lunch?						
have a big breakfast?						
enjoy cooking?						
have dinner parties at home?						

Answer Key

1 = Yes, always   2 = Yes, usually   3 = Yes, sometimes
4 = No, not usually   5 = No, hardly ever   6 = No, never

7

Interview six other people in the class about **sport** and write down their answers. (People may also ask you questions.)

Do you:	1	2	3	4	5	6
play football or any other sport?						
go out and watch sport live?						
do the football pools or bet on horses?						
follow the Olympic Games on TV?						
try to keep fit?						

Answer Key

1 = Yes, always   2 = Yes, usually   3 = Yes, sometimes
4 = No, not usually   5 = No, hardly ever   6 = No, never

8

53 HOW OFTEN DO YOU DO IT?

| Always
Every day
Every *(Monday, month, week, etc.)* | Not very often
Hardly ever
Never |

| Quite often
Sometimes
Only now and again
About *(once, twice)* a *(week, month)* | |

Ask and answer like this:

How often do you (go swimming)?
Always./Hardly ever./etc.

Make statements like these:

I sometimes (play the piano).
I (drive to work) every day.
I (go swimming) quite often.
I don't (eat spaghetti) very often.
I never (go to bed late).
etc.

- -

53   HOW OFTEN DO YOU DO IT? (Part 3)

never	hardly ever	not very often	about once a week
about once a month	about once a year	only now and again	sometimes
quite often	every Monday	every week	every month
every day	always	twice a week	every weekend

go the the cinema	go for a meal at a restaurant	go swimming
play golf	play a musical instrument	listen to pop music
play computer games	write letters	tidy the flat/house
meet new people socially	leave a tip	travel by bus
go abroad	go to the theatre	go for long walks
feel bored	have a party	visit a museum
wear jeans	smoke a cigarette	play cards
listen to classical music	work in the garden	go and see friends
go to parties	listen to the radio	get angry
say something nice to someone	buy clothes	buy records or CDs

54   LIKES AND DISLIKES QUESTIONNAIRE

Complete the sentences below with one of the following words.

love	like	don't really like	hate
really like	quite like	don't like	

1 I _____ going to discos or raves.

2 I _____ playing chess.

3 I _____ meeting new people.

4 I _____ listening to classical music.

5 I _____ flying.

6 I _____ modern art.

7 I _____ babies.

8 I _____ my job (*or my school*).

9 I _____ cats.

10 I _____ being on my own.

11 I _____ doing jigsaw puzzles.

12 I _____ getting up early.

13 I _____ the smell of garlic.

14 I _____ going to the dentist.

15 I _____ walking in the rain.

16 I _____ wearing formal clothes.

17 I _____ being the centre of attention.

18 I _____ new challenges.

19 I _____ doing homework.

20 I _____ family gatherings.

When you have finished, work with a partner. Now talk about your likes and dislikes, e.g.

A: I hate playing chess.
B: Yes, so do I. OR Do you? I don't. I love it.

A: I don't like walking in the rain.
B: No, neither do I. OR Don't you? I do. I really like it.
etc.

Take it in turns to start.

55 ASKING ABOUT LIKES AND DISLIKES

Student A

Work with a partner. Take it in turns to ask and answer questions about your likes and dislikes.
Make a note of whether your partner likes the following:

1 where he/she lives   _____
2 this town/village   _____
3 the leader of his/her government   _____
4 the place where he/she works   _____
   (or the school he/she goes to)
5 watching comedy programmes on TV   _____
6 being with old people   _____
7 driving/cycling   _____
8 eating spaghetti   _____
9 the weather in his/her country   _____
10 doing the ironing   _____

When your partner asks you questions you can answer:

Yes,	I love it/them. very much. I quite like it/them.

No,	not very much. not really. not at all. I hate it/them.

When you have both finished, tell someone else in the class a few things about the person you spoke to. You can say, e.g.

(Carla) loves where she lives. And she quite likes being with old people. But she hates doing the ironing. etc.

Student B

Work with a partner. Take it in turns to ask and answer questions about your likes and dislikes.
Make a note of whether your partner likes the following:

1 modern furniture   _____
2 watching ballet   _____
3 camping   _____
4 learning English   _____
5 playing team sports   _____
6 the smell of cigars or a pipe   _____
7 eating Chinese food   _____
8 going for long walks   _____
9 getting up late at weekends   _____
10 watching horror films (e.g. Dracula)   _____

When your partner asks you questions you can answer:

Yes,	I love it/them. very much. I quite like it/them.

No,	not very much. not really. not at all. I hate it/them.

When you have both finished, tell someone else in the class a few things about the person you spoke to. You can say, e.g.

(Marco) hates modern furniture. And he doesn't really like watching ballet either. But he loves the smell of cigars. etc.

56 WHAT SORT OF A PERSON ARE YOU?

Fill in box 1 on the card below about yourself, then interview five other people in the class. Only tick (✓) the box if they answer YES. (You will also be asked questions.)

Which of these statements apply to you?	1	2	3	4	5	6
I always like to keep my things neat and tidy.						
I am a good listener.						
I am a hard worker.						
I am easily influenced by friends.						
I am usually willing to compromise and cooperate.						
I am good with my hands.						
I am not particularly interested in money.						
I can forget my problems very easily.						
I am musical.						
I enjoy being on my own.						
I find it difficult to admit that I may be wrong.						
I am honest.						

1

- -

Fill in box 1 on the card below about yourself, then interview five other people in the class. Only tick (✓) the box if they answer YES. (You will also be asked questions.)

Which of these statements apply to you?	1	2	3	4	5	6
I am ambitious.						
I am usually calm and not easily upset.						
I am fashion-conscious.						
I am often afraid that I may look ridiculous or make a fool of myself.						
I am satisfied with my appearance.						
I am superstitious.						
I enjoy eating good food.						
I can relax quite easily.						
I enjoy being the centre of attention.						
I find it hard to talk to strangers.						
I find that my first impression of a person is usually correct.						
I get upset if someone criticizes me.						

2

Fill in box 1 on the card below about yourself, then interview five other people in the class. Only tick (✓) the box if they answer YES. (You will also be asked questions.)

Which of these statements apply to you?	1	2	3	4	5	6
I am concerned about my appearance.						
I am essentially very cautious, conventional and conservative.						
I am impulsive.						
I am sure of myself.						
I am very attached to my family and friends.						
I am very good at hiding my true feelings.						
I feel anxious when I speak in front of a large group.						
I find it difficult to say no.						
I have a tendency to give up easily when I meet a difficult problem.						
I love a challenge and function best under stress.						
On the whole I am a very optimistic person.						
I often help other people.						

3

- -

Fill in box 1 on the card below about yourself, then interview five other people in the class. Only tick (✓) the box if they answer YES. (You will also be asked questions.)

Which of these statements apply to you?	1	2	3	4	5	6
I am interested in the latest fashion.						
I am optimistic.						
I am very faithful to my friends and always keep promises.						
I am very practical by nature.						
I feel embarrassed when looking at photographs of myself.						
I frequently suffer from insomnia.						
I get upset if things don't go according to plan.						
I like to share my problems with my friends.						
I often worry that I will do or say the wrong thing.						
I prefer to be at home rather than go to parties.						
I work best in a team.						
I am self-confident.						

4

56 WHAT SORT OF A PERSON ARE YOU? (continued)

Fill in box 1 on the card below about yourself, then interview five other people in the class. Only tick (✓) the box if they answer YES. (You will also be asked questions.)

Which of these statements apply to you?	1	2	3	4	5	6
I am shy and self-conscious in social situations.						
I am very careful about the way I dress.						
I am warm-hearted and usually generous to others.						
I care very much if people like me or not.						
I get embarrassed very easily.						
I frequently suffer from insomnia.						
I like to work by myself in my own way.						
I love luxury, beauty and pleasure.						
I often think 'I wish I were a child again.'						
I prefer eating good food in style rather than grabbing a quick meal.						
I prefer to listen than to talk.						
I sometimes have difficulty controlling my temper.						

5

- -

Fill in box 1 on the card below about yourself, then interview five other people in the class. Only tick (✓) the box if they answer YES. (You will also be asked questions.)

Which of these statements apply to you?	1	2	3	4	5	6
One of my main aims in life is to do something that will make my parents proud of me.						
Once I have made my mind up I seldom change it.						
I prefer to stay in the background rather than push myself forward.						
I tend to be very lucky.						
It's difficult to find anything to talk about when I meet a new person.						
Large groups of people make me nervous.						
I get easily upset by things.						
I usually end up making the decisions when I am with a group.						
I love nothing better than a challenge.						
I try to get my own way.						
I don't really worry about what others think of me.						
I sometimes have difficulty controlling my temper.						

6

Work in groups of 5–8. Think of the people in the group then, working alone, fill in the missing words in the sentences below. Choose from the following:

> All of us/Everyone
> Most of us
> Some of us
> Only a few of us
> Hardly any of us
> None of us/No one

		How many?	Correct?
1 _____	has/have been in hospital.	____	____
2 _____	has/have visited a Scandinavian country.	____	____
3 _____	has/have been seasick.	____	____
4 _____	has/have been to the USA.	____	____
5 _____	has/have been to a circus as a child.	____	____
6 _____	has/have broken the speed-limit.	____	____
7 _____	has/have stayed up the whole night.	____	____
8 _____	has/have eaten goat's cheese.	____	____
9 _____	has/have had a penfriend.	____	____
10 _____	has/have acted in a play or sung in a musical.	____	____
11 _____	has/have spoken to someone from Wales or Scotland.	____	____
12 _____	has/have smoked a pipe or cigar.	____	____
13 _____	has/have driven a car really fast.	____	____
14 _____	has/have failed a test or an exam.	____	____
15 _____	has/have made a personal call from work.	____	____
16 _____	has/have eaten real caviare.	____	____
17 _____	has/have sent back food at a restaurant.	____	____
18 _____	has/have won money in a raffle or competition.	____	____
19 _____	has/have tried to smuggle something through Customs after a holiday.	____	____
20 _____	has/have made a speech in public.	____	____

When you have finished, check to see how accurate you were by taking it in turns to ask each other in the group if they have ever done the above things.

Q	**Disagree** 1	2	3	4	5	6	7	8	9	**Agree** 10
1										
2										
3										
4										
5										
6										
7										
8										
9										
10										
11										
12										
13										
14										
15										

---

58 WHAT DO YOU THINK? (teacher's sheet)

Read out the following:

1 Men and women can never really be equal. (EQUALITY)
2 The most important thing about a job is the money you earn. (MONEY)
3 You should look after your parents when they are old, even if this means one or more of your parents living with you. (PARENTS)
4 Most people in my country are prejudiced towards foreigners, but few will admit it. (PREJUDICED)
5 It isn't very important if you make a mistake in English as long as people understand you. (MISTAKES)
6 It is acceptable for a man to marry a woman much younger than himself, but not for a woman to do so. (MARRY)
7 The Women's Liberation Movement has caused as many problems as it has solved. (WOMEN'S LIB)
8 It is impossible to have a successful career and a successful family life. You have to choose one or the other. (CHOOSE)
9 People suffering from incurable diseases should have the choice of being put painlessly to death. (DEATH)
10 We should try to cure criminals not punish them. (CRIMINALS)
11 No one nowadays should be allowed to have more than one car and one child. (ONLY ONE)
12 Watching violent videos makes young people aggressive. (VIDEOS)
13 Getting married and having children is more important for a woman than a man. (CHILDREN)
14 A Third World War is inevitable. (WAR)
15 Pop singers, filmstars and sportsmen and women don't deserve all the money they earn. (STARS)

59 CAN YOU FOLLOW INSTRUCTIONS?

*The following test is to see how well you can follow instructions. But you **only have 5 minutes** in which to complete it so you will have to work quickly. Have a pen or pencil ready and begin when your teacher says 'Start'. You must stop immediately when your teacher says 'Time's up!' You must not talk to anyone else in the class or let them see your paper. Good luck!*

1 Read through the questions carefully first.

2 Write your surname in the left-hand box above.

3 Draw a circle around the word *surname* in sentence two.

4 Draw two small triangles in the right-hand box above.

5 Put an 'X' inside each triangle.

6 Put a circle around each triangle.

7 Write your first name in the middle box above.

8 Write *Yes, I can* after the title.

9 Put a circle around the word *follow* in the title.

10 Underline sentence 5.

11 Multiply 123 by 76 and write your answer in the following box:

12 Underline the seventh word in sentence 4.

13 When you reach this sentence, stand up, clap your hands twice then sit down again.

14 Write your teacher's name in this box:

15 Cross out the second word in the sentence which begins with the word *Read*.

16 Draw a tree in the box in the bottom right-hand corner of the page.

17 Draw a picture of the sun above the tree you have just drawn.

18 When you reach this sentence, say out loud *I have reached sentence eighteen!*

19 Count up all the words in the first three sentences. Write the total in the following circle:

20 Put a circle around every *the* in the first ten sentences.

21 Find the word *carefully* in one of the sentences and underline it.

22 When you reach this sentence, walk to the door, touch it and say, *I have almost finished.*

23 Cross out all the odd numbers in front of each sentence.

24 Now that you have read through all the sentences, just write your name here:

60   COMPLETE THE DRAWING
Student A

Your partner has an incomplete version of the following drawing.

cloud

sun

birds
mountain

river

trees

road

smoke
chimney

bridge

windows
curtains

man fishing

door

trees

grass

dog

Help your partner to complete it by telling him/her what to draw and where to draw it. You can look at your partner's paper but you must not touch or point to anything or let him/her see your drawing. (The words around the drawing are only to help you. Your partner doesn't need to write these down.)

When you have finished, compare your drawings.

© Penguin Books 1995

---

60   COMPLETE THE DRAWING
Student B

The following drawing is not complete. There are several things missing. Your partner has a completed version of the drawing and is going to tell you how to complete yours. You are allowed to ask him/her questions, but you mustn't look at his/her paper. Before you start, make sure you know what these words mean:

bird	cloud	door	mountain	smoke
bridge	curtains	fishing	river	tree
chimney	dog	grass	road	window

When you have finished, compare your drawings.

© Penguin Books 1995   111

Student A

Read the following out to your partner. He/she is going to draw what you tell him/her to draw. (Don't let him/her see your paper.)

1	2	3	4	5	6
7	8	9	10	11	12
13	14	15	16	17	18
19	20	21	22	23	24
25	26	27	28	29	30

1 Start in the square above the picture of a flower.

2 Go left 2 squares, then down 2 squares. In this square copy the picture in the square below.

3 Go right 4 squares and copy the picture in the square on your left.

4 Go up 2 squares, then left 1 square. In this square copy the picture in the square above.

5 Go left 3 squares then right 2 squares. In this square copy the picture in the square below.

6 Go down 2 squares then left 3 squares. In this square copy the picture in the square above.

Now check your drawings.

ANSWER

Now it's your turn to listen to instructions. Have a pen or pencil ready. Follow your partner's instructions and draw what he/she tells you to draw. When you have finished, check drawings.

Student B

Have a pen ready to follow your partner's instructions and to draw what he/she tells you to draw.

When you have finished, check your drawings. But hide the bottom part of your paper from Student A.

1	2	3	4	5	6
7	8	9	10	11	12
13	14	15	16	17	18
19	20	21	22	23	24
25	26	27	28	29	30

Now it is your turn to give your partner instructions. Read out the following. He/she is going to draw what you tell him/her to draw.

1 Start in the square below the house.
2 Go down 2 squares, then left 1 square. In this square copy the picture in the square on your left.
3 Go left 2 squares, then up 2 squares. In this square copy the picture in the square on your right.
4 Go down 1 square, then right 4 squares. In this square copy the picture in the square on your left.
5 Go down 1 square, then left 5 squares. In this square, copy the picture in the square above.
6 Go up 3 squares, then right 3 squares. In this square copy the picture in the square on your left.

Now check your drawings.

ANSWER

1	2	3	4	5	6
7	8	9	10	11	12
13	14	15	16	17	18
19	20	21	22	23	24
25	26	27	28	29	30

Student A

Fill in the following on your answer sheet.

1 In square number 2, write tomorrow's date.
2 In square number 4, write your first name.
3 In square number 6, write what year it is.
4 In square number 8, write the colour of your shoes.
5 In square number 14, write the number 7,537.
6 In square number 17, write the name of the capital of Japan.
7 In square number 23, write your teacher's surname.
8 In square number 25, write what day it is today.

Now work with your partner. He/she has a 25-square blank rectangle. Help him/her to fill in 18 of them by reading out loud the following instructions. But do not let him/her see your answer sheet.

1 Start in the square below the black square. Go right 2 squares then up 1 square. Draw a picture of a lamp in this square.
2 Go down 3 squares, then right 1 square. Write which day it is today in this square.
3 Go left 3 squares. Draw a picture of an apple in this square, and in the square on the right your teacher's surname.
4 Go back to the black square. Go up 1 square and write tomorrow's date. Then, in the square on your left draw a comb and in the square on your right draw a triangle.
5 Go to the square to the right of the apple. Go up 2 squares, then right 1 square. Write the number 7, 537 in this square.
6 Go left 3 squares and draw a picture of a pair of scissors and in the square below this a picture of a clock.
7 Go to the square in the top right-hand corner and draw a picture of a candle.
8 Go down 3 squares, then left 3 squares. In this square write the name of the capital of Japan.
9 Go up 2 squares, then left 1 square. In this square write what year it is.
10 Go to the square under the candle. Go left 2 squares, then down 1 square. Draw a picture of a fish in this square and in the square above write the colour of my shoes.
11 Go to the square in the bottom left-hand corner. Go right 3 squares. Draw a picture of a cross in this square.
12 Go up 4 squares and write my first name in this square.
13 Finally, go right 1 square, go down 2 squares, go left 3 squares, go down 1 square again and then go right 3 squares. In this square draw a picture of a chair.

When you have finished, compare rectangles.

1	2	3	4	5
6	7	8	9	10
11	12	13	14	15
16	17	18	19	20
21	22	23	24	25

62   UP, DOWN, LEFT, RIGHT 2

Student B

Here is a rectangle with 25 squares. You are going to write or draw something in 18 of them. Your partner will tell you what to write or draw. You are allowed to ask your partner questions, but you must not ask him/her for the number of the square you are to write or draw in.

1	2	3	4	5
6	7	8	9	10
11	12	13	14	15
16	17	18	19	20
21	22	23	24	25

When you have finished, compare rectangles to see if you filled in everything correctly.

63 TAKING A GROUP PHOTOGRAPH (photo 1)

Imagine you are a photographer. Arrange the five people in your group so that they look like the following drawing:

When you have finshed, ask your teacher to give you a mark out of ten for your 'photograph'.

63 TAKING A GROUP PHOTOGRAPH (photo 2)

Imagine you are a photographer. Arrange the five people in your group so that they look like the following drawing:

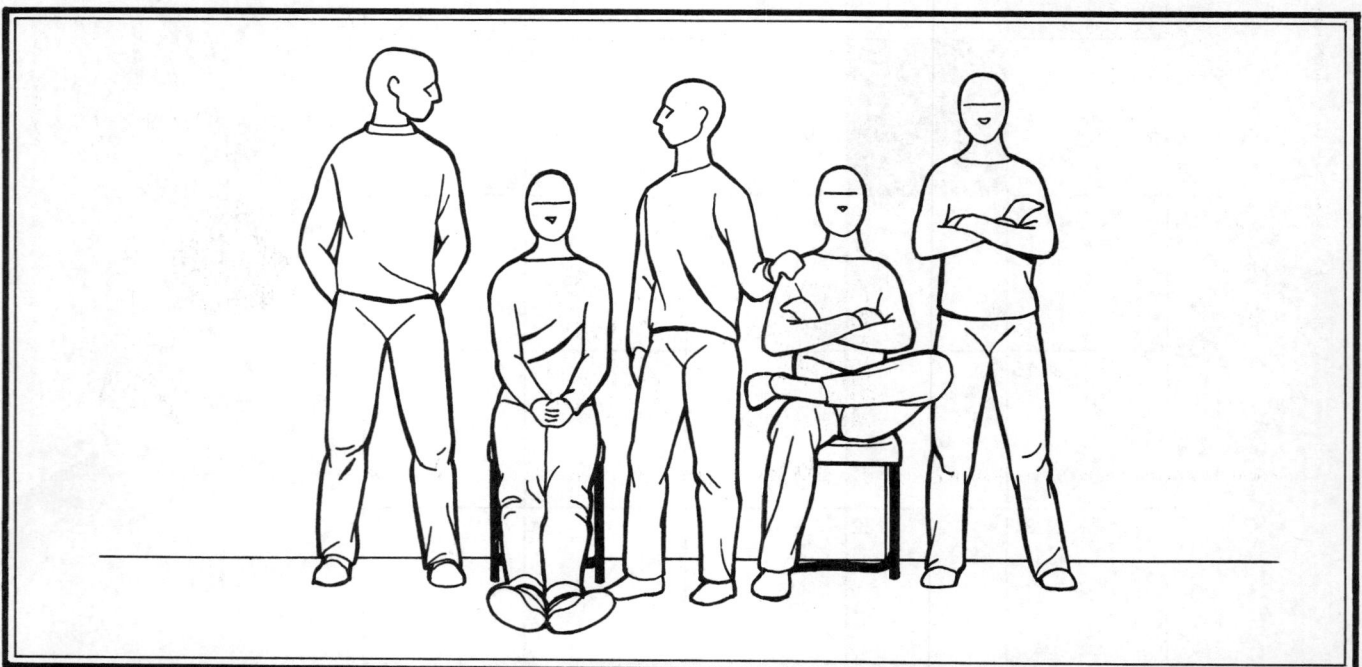

When you have finished, ask your teacher to give you a mark out of ten for your 'photograph'.

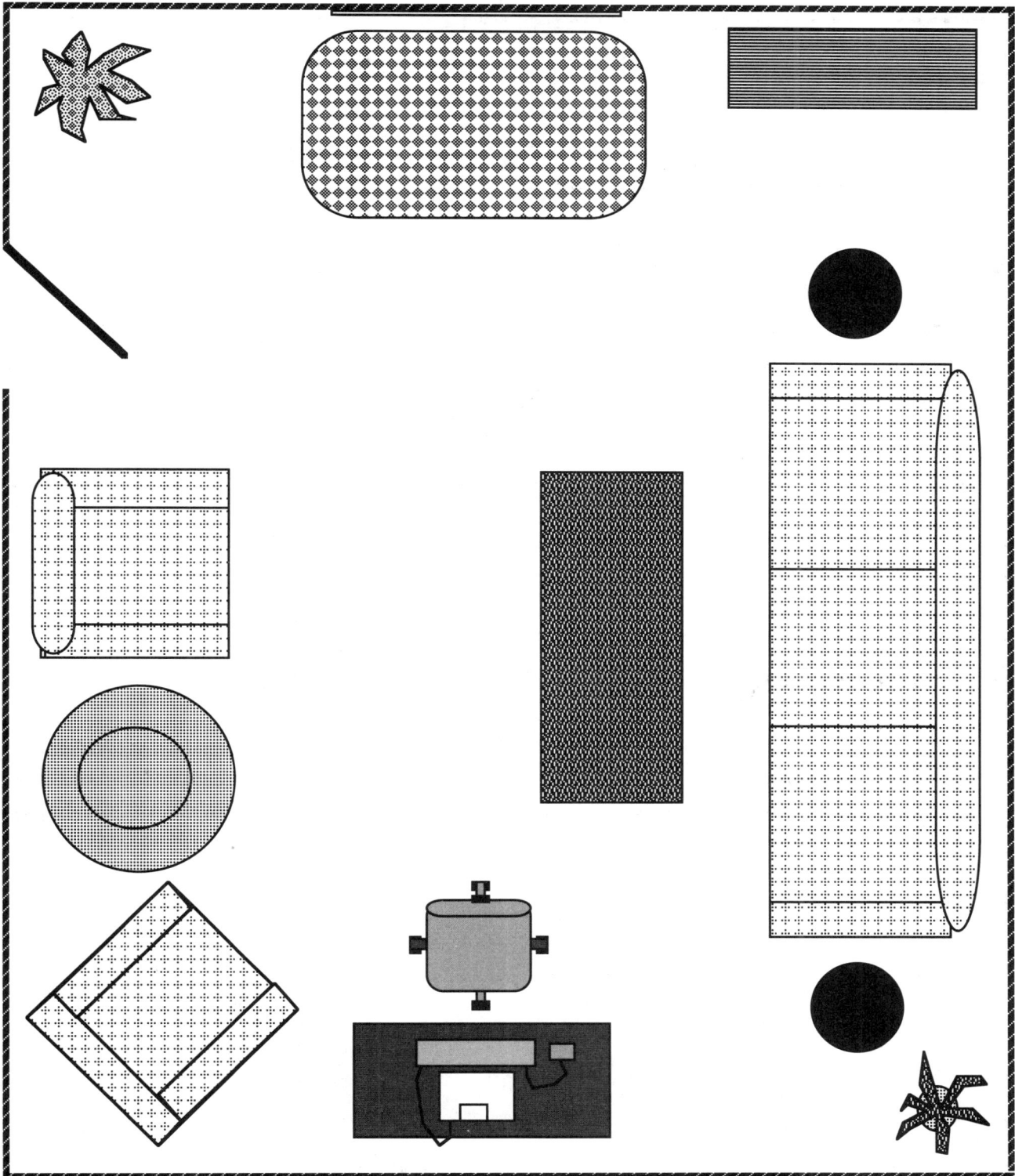

Top

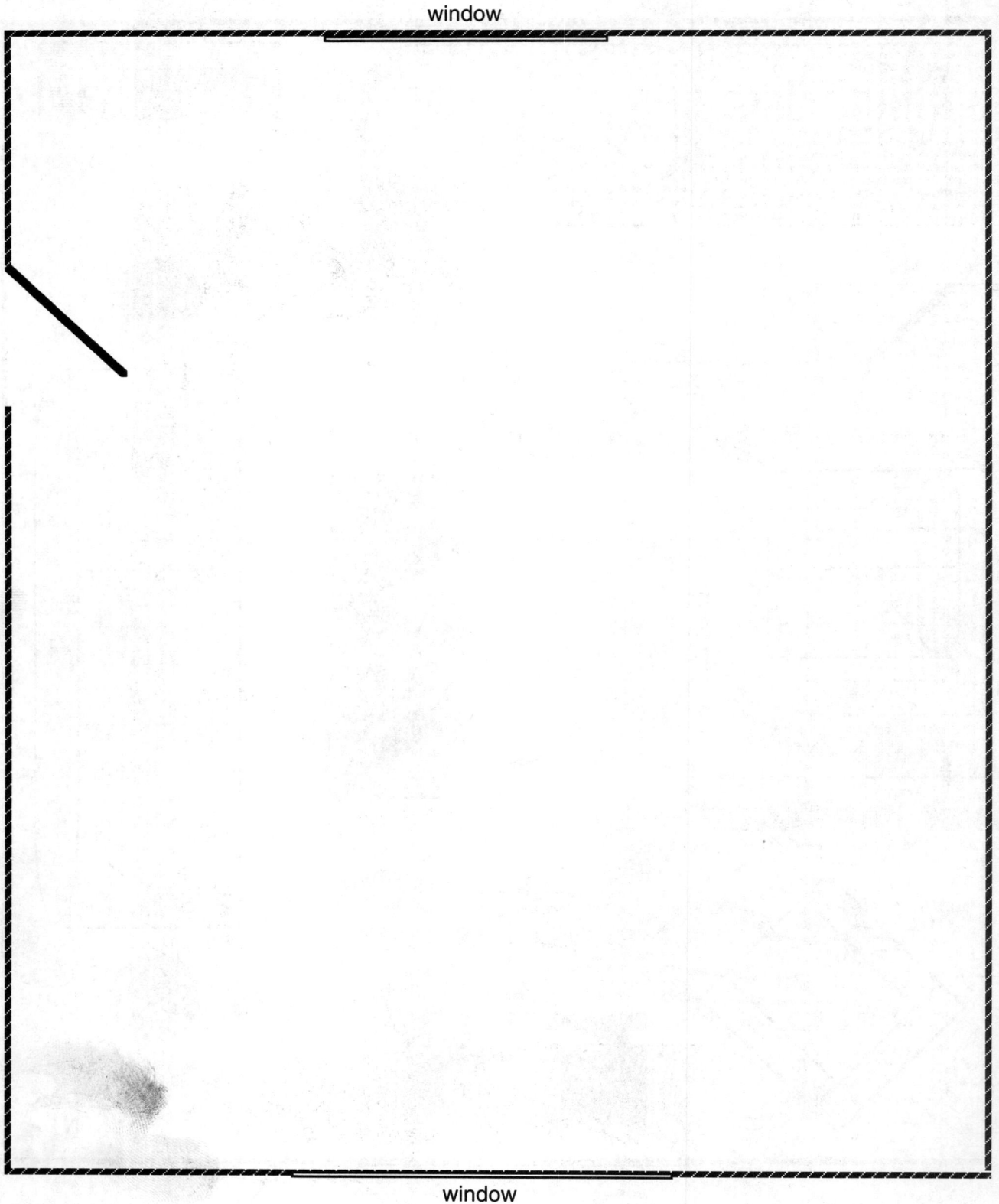

Top

window

window

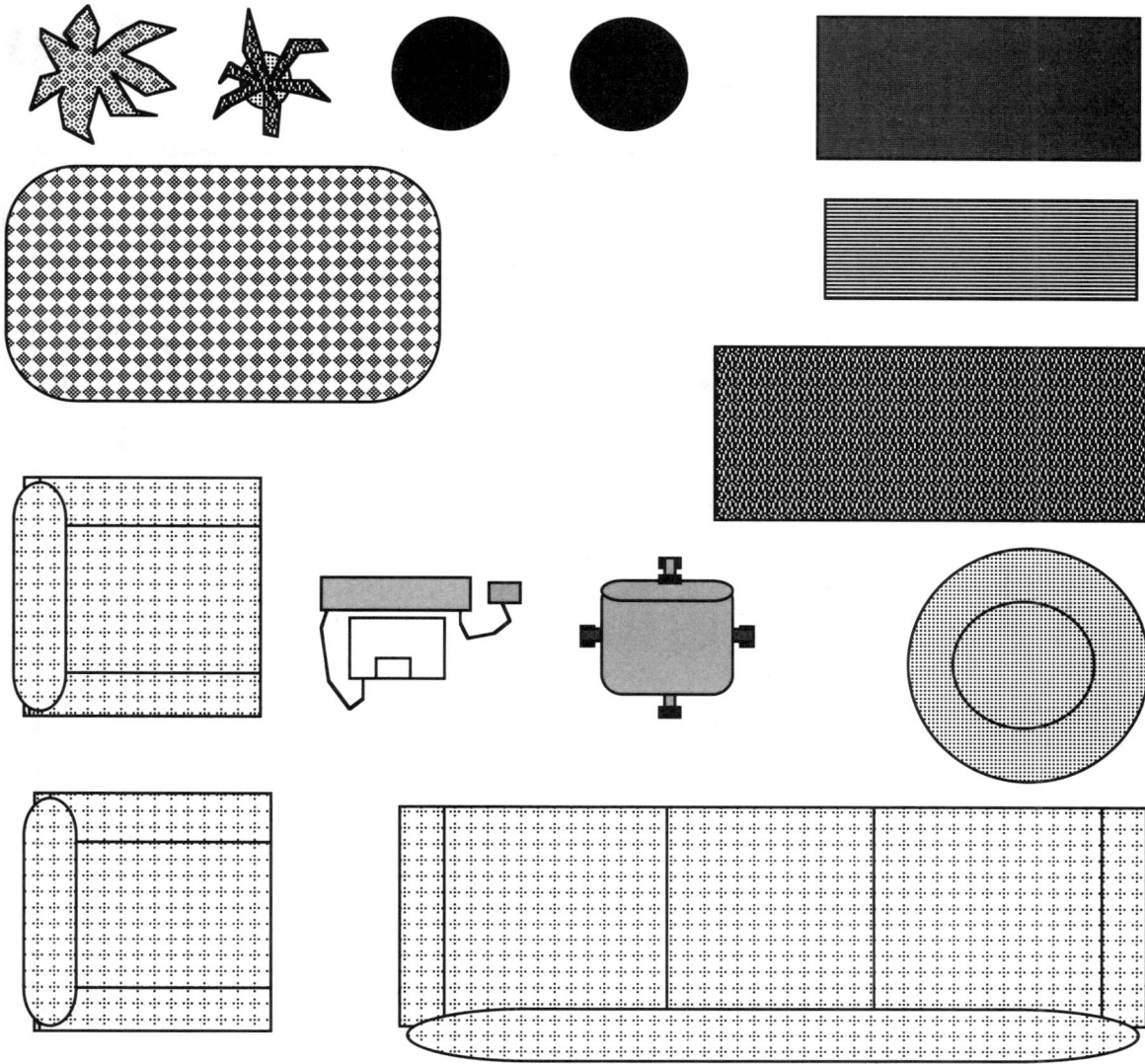

64/65   ARRANGE THE FURNITURE (Key)

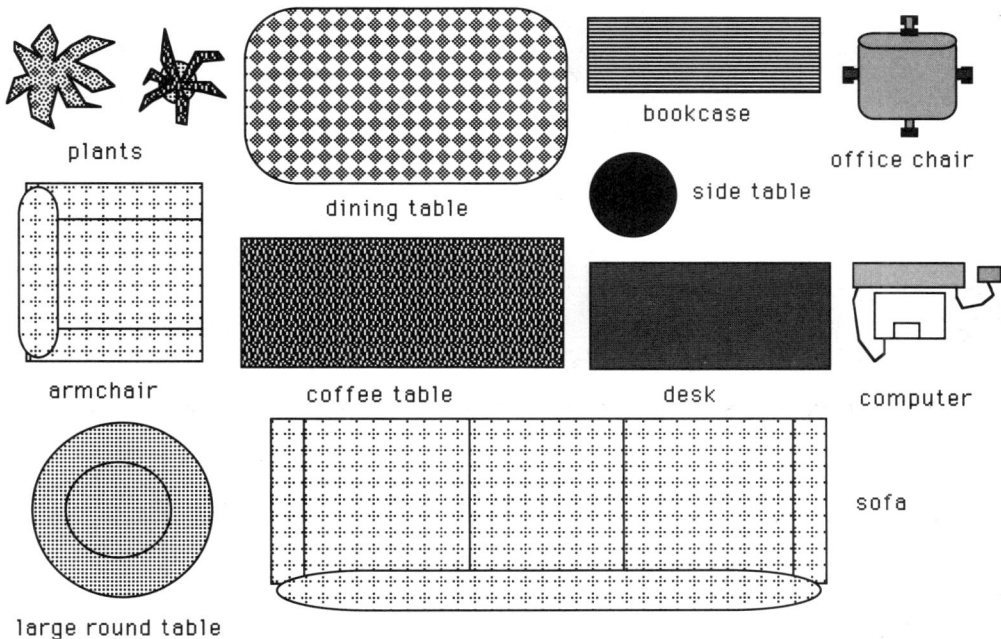

plants

dining table

bookcase

office chair

side table

armchair

coffee table

desk

computer

sofa

large round table

Top

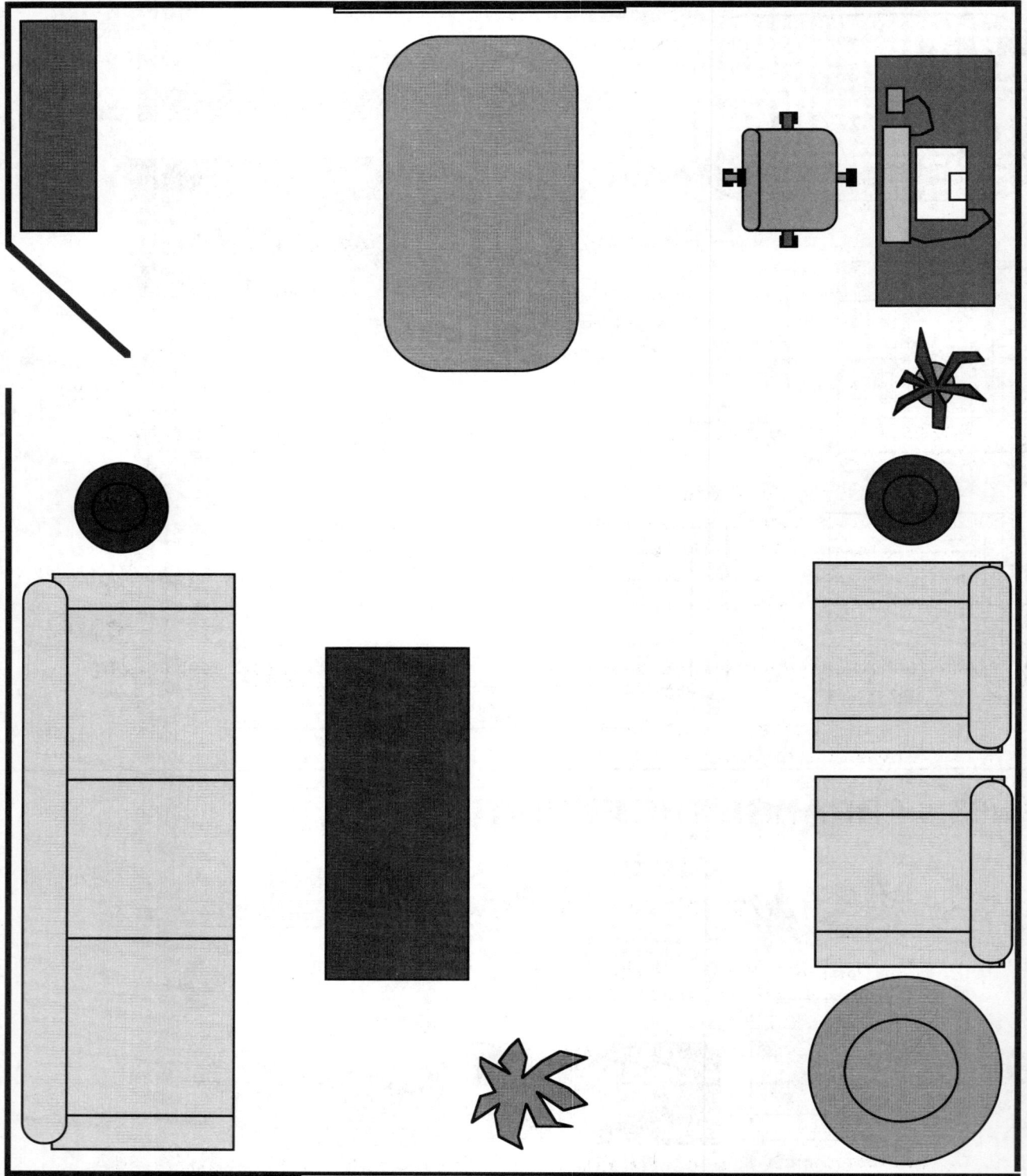

65 ARRANGE THE FURNITURE 2 (Group cards)

CARD 1
CARD 1

You can read out the following, but you must not let anyone else see your card or write anything down.

1   The bookcase is behind the door.
2   The dining table is in front of the window.
3   The desk is in the corner, opposite the door.
4   The sofa is in the corner.

CARD 2

You can read out the following, but you must not let anyone else see your card or write anything down.

1   The bookcase is against the wall, facing the dining table.
2   The side tables are opposite each other.
3   The coffee table is in front of the sofa.
4   The two armchairs are next to the large round table.

CARD 3

You can read out the following, but you must not let anyone else see your card or write anything down.

1   The long end of the dining table is parallel to the door.
2   The office chair is in front of the desk.
3   There is a plant between one of the side tables and the desk.
4   As you open the door to leave the room, the bookcase is facing you on your right.

CARD 4

You can read out the following, but you must not let anyone else see your card or write anything down.

1   One of the side tables is next to the sofa, near the door.
2   The sofa is opposite the armchairs.
3   As you enter the room, the long round table is in the right-hand corner.
4   The sofa is not against any of the walls with windows.

CARD 5

You can read out the following, but you must not let anyone else see your card or write anything down.

1   The computer is on the desk.
2   The dining table is near the door.
3   One of the plants is in the middle of the window.
4   The two armchairs are next to each other.

CARD 6

You can read out the following, but you must not let anyone else see your card or write anything down.

1   As you enter the room, the sofa is immediately on your right.
2   One of the side tables is next to one of the armchairs.
3   There is a plant between the sofa and the large round table.
4   The armchairs are against the wall opposite the door.

66   THE ADVERB GAME (list of adverbs)

accurately	affectionately	aggressively	angrily
anxiously	arrogantly	badly	calmly
carefully	carelessly	casually	cautiously
cheerfully	clumsily	confidently	energetically
furiously	gently	gracefully	happily
indifferently	loudly	lovingly	nervously
noisily	nonchalantly	passionately	playfully
proudly	quickly	quietly	reluctantly
sadly	self-consciously	sensuously	seriously
sexily	shyly	silently	sleepily
slowly	smugly	stiffly	stylishly
superstitiously	suspiciously	tensely	timidly
violently	wearily	well	wildly

eat an apple	put on a pair of jeans	play football
drink a cup of coffee	walk on a tightrope	do a tap dance
drive a car	do the ironing	dial a phone number
stroke a dog	knock in a nail	do the washing-up
hit a golf ball	mow the lawn	clean the windows
eat spaghetti	kiss your grandmother	brush your teeth
sing a song	have a shower	sit down
play the piano	blow your nose	make the bed
take off your shoes	comb your hair	light a cigarette
post a letter	lick an envelope	dig the garden

Student A

On the map below is a route which starts from the station and ends at the library. Your partner has a blank map. Help him/her to trace the same route as yours. You are not allowed to show him your map or to point at anything on his/hers.

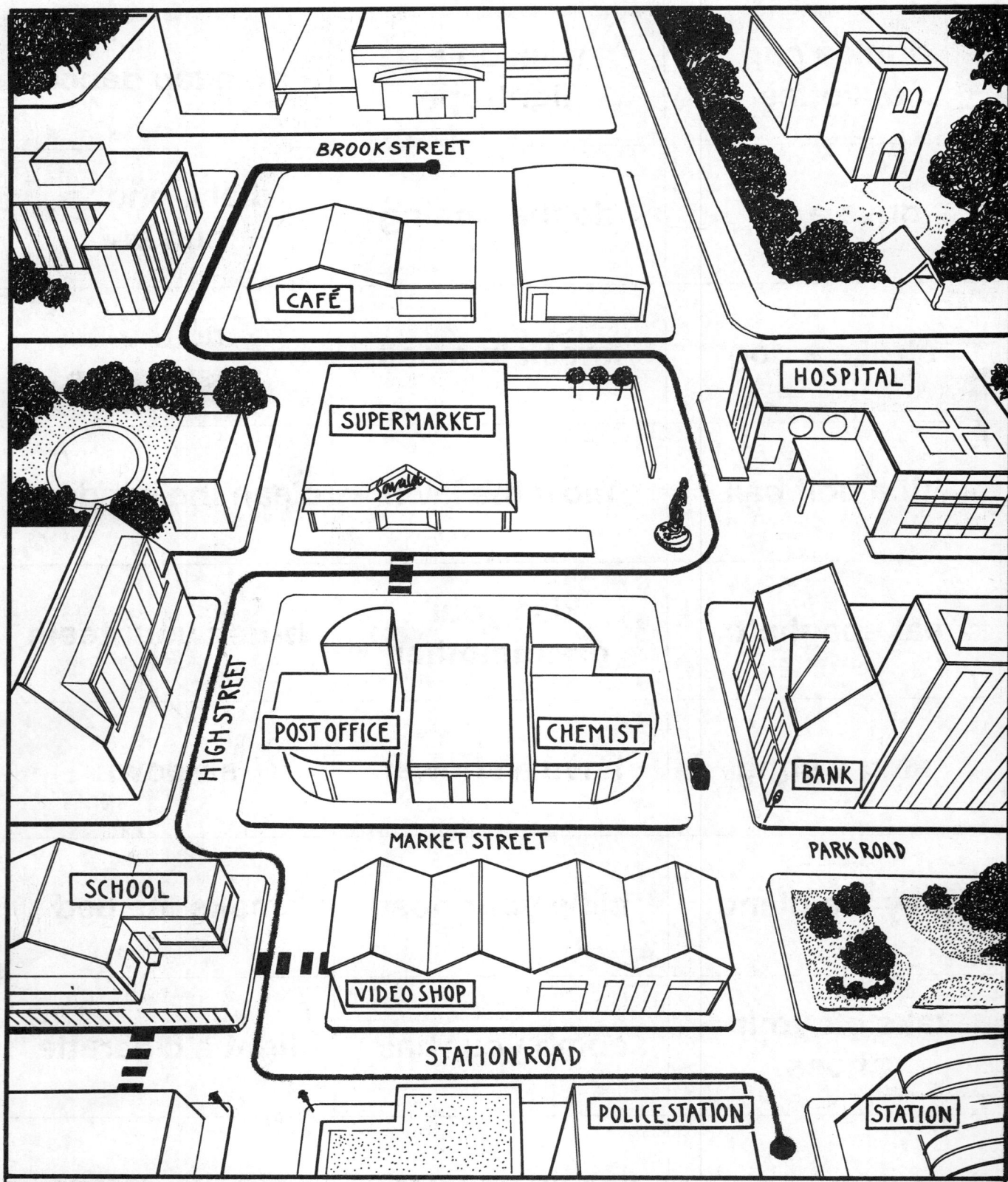

When you have finished, compare maps.

© Penguin Books 1995

67 TRACE THE ROUTE

Student B

Your partner is going to ask you to trace a route which starts at the station and ends somewhere else. Have a pencil ready to mark the route and write down the name of the building you finish at. You can ask your partner questions but you are not allowed to look at his/her map.

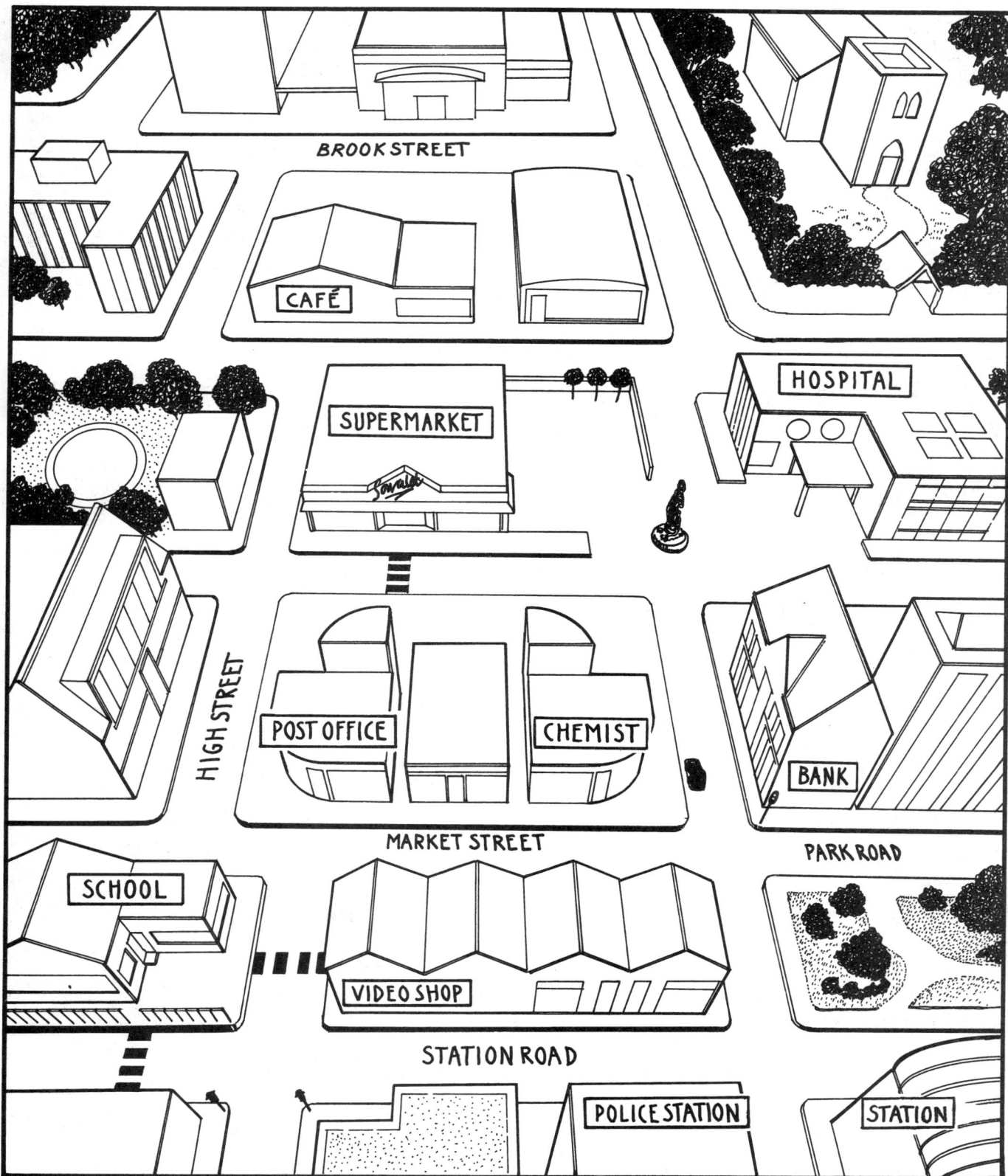

When you have finished, compare maps.

68 THE AUDITION

Producer

Imagine you are a producer of TV commercials. You are soon going to be making a commercial for cat food. The script is ready, you just need to find an actor/actress now. Your partner is an actor/actress who has applied for the part in the commercial. He/she has been sent a script of the words to say. Get him/her to run through the script, using the notes you have made on the following storyboard to give him/her exact instructions as to how you want everything done.

Get person to mime opening a tin of cat food...

...and then to turn to face the camera before starting to speak.

VOICE
(Look straight into the camera.)
As a champion cat breeder, I know what my cats need to make them strong and healthy, *(slight pause here)* to make them champions.

Mime holding up the tin of CLAWS.

VOICE
And so I always give them CLAWS – the cat food with delicious meaty chunks of liver.

Mime emptying the tin into 3 bowls on the floor.

VOICE
My cats just love it!

Mime walking to the door and opening it.

VOICE
(Shouting)
Mimi! Suzie! Captain Silver! Hamlet! Agatha!

Mime following the cats' movements as they rush through the door and crowd around the bowls of food.

Then turn to face the camera again.

VOICE
See what I mean!

Mime holding up the tin of CLAWS again.

VOICE
So take my advice and give your cats CLAWS. It will make champions out of them!

Give a big smile and hold it for as long as possible.

126 © Penguin Books 1995

68 THE AUDITION

Actor/actress

Imagine you are an actor/actress who has applied for a part in a TV commercial about cat food. You have been sent the followiong script and are about to be auditioned by the producer (your partner). Try to do what he/she says.

Script for CLAWS cat food commericial

VOICE

As a champion cat breeder, I know what my cats need to make them strong and healthy, to make them champions.

And so I always give them CLAWS – the cat food with delicious meaty chunks of liver.

My cats just love it!

Mimi! Suzie! Captain Silver! Hamlet! Agatha!

See what I mean!

So take my advice and give your cats CLAWS. It will make champions out of them!

NUMBERS 1–20 (For Activities 69–71)

1	2	3	4
5	6	7	8
9	10	11	12
13	14	15	16
17	18	19	20

break [1]	**buy** [2]	**drink** [3]	**drive** [4]
eat [5]	**find** [6]	**fly** [7]	**forget** [8]
learn [9]	**leave** [10]	**lose** [11]	**make** [12]
meet [13]	**sell** [14]	**send** [15]	**shoot** [16]
sing [17]	**speak** [18]	**spend** [19]	**write** [20]

1 the first time you went abroad	**2** your first car	**3** a relative	**4** one of your best friends at school
5 a party you really enjoyed	**6** your grandparents	**7** an important event from your childhood *(first or last day at school, moving home, etc.)*	**8** your last holiday
9 a teacher at school you either liked a lot or hated a lot	**10** the town or village where you grew up	**11** your first boyfriend, girlfriend or love *(choose)*	**12** a place where you used to spend the summer as a child
13 what you used to do at weekends when you were a teenager	**14** one of your best friends at school	**15** your first job *(or first summer job)*	**16** your wedding day *(or someone else's)*
17 your first *(or favourite)* house/flat	**18** an experience that was either frightening or embarrassing	**19** a hobby you used to have	**20** a holiday you didn't enjoy very much

1 The saddest thing I ever saw…	**2** If I only had three months left to live…	**3** I wish my parents were less… and more…	**4** I still haven't…
5 My (brother, mother, etc.) gets angry if…	**6** Two things that really give me pleasure are … and …	**7** Right now I'd like to…	**8** I feel happiest when…
9 Parents should never…	**10** I hate people who…	**11** In the next 5 years I'm going to…	**12** If I could foretell the future I'd…
13 If I were an animal I'd like to be a/an… because…	**14** The thing that worries me most about the world today…	**15** The one place I'd really like to visit…	**16** I wish teachers would…
17 This country would be a better place to live in if…	**18** If I won £1 million I'd…	**19** People should try to…	**20** I hardly ever…

72 FOUR-IN-A-ROW: VERBS

1 be	2 begin	3 bite	4 blow	5 break
6 bring	7 build	8 buy	9 catch	10 choose
11 come	12 cost	13 cut	14 do	15 draw
16 drink	17 drive	18 eat	19 fall	20 find
21 fly	22 forget	23 freeze	24 get	25 give
26 go	27 grow	28 hear	29 hide	30 hit
31 know	32 lay	33 leave	34 lie	35 make
36 meet	37 pay	38 read	39 ride	40 rise
41 run	42 say	43 sell	44 show	45 shrink
46 sing	47 speak	48 stand	49 steal	50 write

73 FOUR-IN-A-ROW: PREPOSITIONS (after adjectives/verbs)

1 accuse (vb)	2 addicted (adj)	3 advertise (vb)	4 afraid (adj)	5 agree (vb)
6 allergic (adj)	7 amazed (adj)	8 angry (adj)	9 apologize (vb)	10 apply (vb)
11 argue (vb)	12 aware (adj)	13 bad (adj)	14 believe (vb)	15 belong (adj)
16 boast (vb)	17 bored (adj)	18 borrow (vb)	19 capable (adj)	20 co-operate (vb)
21 confide (vb)	22 content (adj)	23 deal (vb)	24 decide (vb)	25 differ (vb)
26 disappointed (adj)	27 disapprove (vb)	28 famous (adj)	29 fluent (adj)	30 full (adj)
31 hope (vb)	32 insist (vb)	33 insured (adj)	34 interested (adj)	35 jealous (adj)
36 make fun vb)	37 married (adj)	38 multiply (vb)	39 popular (adj)	40 recover (vb)
41 rely (vb)	42 responsible (adj)	43 satisfied (adj)	44 similar (adj)	45 suffer (vb)
46 suspicious (adj)	47 tired (adj)	48 translate (vb)	49 vote (vb)	50 worried (adj)

72 FOUR-IN-A-ROW: VERBS (Key)

1	be	was	been	26	go	went	gone
2	begin	began	begun	27	grow	grew	grown
3	bite	bit	bitten	28	hear	heard	heard
4	blow	blew	blown	29	hide	hid	hidden
5	break	broke	broken	30	hit	hit	hit
6	bring	brought	brought	31	know	knew	known
7	build	built	built	32	lay	laid	laid
8	buy	bought	bought	33	leave	left	left
9	catch	caught	caught	34	lie	lay	lain
10	choose	chose	chosen	35	make	made	made
11	come	came	come	36	meet	met	met
12	cost	cost	cost	37	pay	paid	paid
13	cut	cut	cut	38	read	read [red]	read [red]
14	do	did	done	39	ride	rode	ridden
15	draw	drew	drawn	40	rise	rose	risen
16	drink	drank	drunk	41	run	ran	run
17	drive	drove	driven	42	say	said	said
18	eat	ate	eaten	43	sell	sold	sold
19	fall	fell	fallen	44	show	showed	shown
20	find	found	found	45	shrink	shrank	shrunk
21	fly	flew	flown	46	sing	sang	sung
22	forget	forgot	forgotten	47	speak	spoke	spoken
23	freeze	froze	frozen	48	stand	stood	stood
24	get	got	got	49	steal	stole	stolen
25	give	gave	given	50	write	wrote	written

- -

73 FOUR-IN-A-ROW: PREPOSITIONS (after adjectives/verbs) Key

1 accuse *(someone)* of *(doing something)*
2 addicted to *(something)*
3 advertise for *(something)* in *(a newspaper)*
4 afraid of *(someone or something)*
5 agree with *(someone)*
6 allergic to *(a substance)*
7 amazed at/by *(something)*
8 angry at/about *(something)*
   angry with *(someone)*
9 apologize for *(something)*
10 apply for *(a job)*
11 argue with *(someone)*
12 aware of *(something)*
13 bad at *(doing something)*
   bad for *(someone)*
14 believe in *(something)*
15 belong to *(a person, organization)*
16 boast about/of *(something)*
17 bored with *(something)*
18 borrow from/off *(someone)*
19 capable of *(doing something)*
20 co-operate with *(someone)*
21 confide in *(someone)*
22 content with *(something)*
23 deal with *(someone)*
24 decide on/upon *(something)*
25 differ from *(something else)*

26 disappointed in/at *(something)*
   disappointed in/with *(someone)*
27 disapprove of *(something or someone)*
28 famous for *(something)*
29 fluent in *(a language)*
30 full of *(something)*
31 hope for *(something)*
32 insist on/upon *(doing or having something)*
33 insured against *(something bad that might happen)*
34 interested in *(something)*
35 jealous of *(someone)*
36 make fun of *(someone)*
37 married to *(someone)*
38 multiply *(one mumber)* by *(another)*
39 popular with *(a person or group of people)*
40 recover from *(an illness or an unpleasant experience)*
41 rely on/upon *(someone)*
42 responsible to *(someone)* for *(something)*
43 satisfied with *(something)*
44 similar to *(something else)*
45 suffer from *(a disease or illness)*
46 suspicious of *(someone or something)*
47 tired of *(something or someone)*
48 translate from *(one language)* into *(another)*
49 vote for/against *(something)*
50 worried about *(something)*

Start here							**Start here**
by	at	■	between	for	in	with	on
in	to	from	about	at	■	from	about
■	with	by	for	on	during	at	in
from	during	on	■	between	about	with	■
on	■	at	during	■	in	for	from
to	by	in	on	from	about	■	to
at	between	■	with	for	on	by	during
Start here	in	for	by	to	between	■	at	about
							Start here

© Penguin Books 1995

74 THE PREPOSITION GAME (students' cards)

CARD 1

1 Tell me something _____ where you live.

2 I'll see you _____ 10.30.

3 Shall we go to the cinema _____ Tuesday?

4 She was born _____ October.

5 There was a snowstorm _____ the night.

6 Sweden lies _____ Norway and Finland.

7 I bought this watch _____ only £5.

8 They went to Scotland _____ train.

CARD 2

1 Where does James come _____?

2 We always walk _____ work.

3 Would you like a piece of cake _____ your coffee?

4 Did Sally tell you _____ her new job?

5 We usually stay in _____ night.

6 The plates are _____ the top shelf.

7 He usually gets up at 7.30 _____ the morning.

8 She was so tired that she fell asleep _____ the film.

CARD 3

1 We went to France _____ boat.

2 The town of Eastbourne lies _____ Hastings and Brighton.

3 I met Paul _____ the station.

4 She sat _____ a stool.

5 He arrived _____ Mexico last week.

6 She bought the dress _____ only £20.

7 We walked _____ the hotel to the beach.

8 Who's that woman over there _____ glasses?

CARD 4

1 We're going _____ Majorca next week.

2 He talks _____ golf all the time!

3 She met her husband _____ a party.

4 My flat is _____ the third floor.

5 The Eiffel Tower is _____ Paris.

6 This play is _____ Shakespeare.

7 We worked _____ 6 o'clock to midnight.

8 "I will love you _____ ever!" he said to her.

75 BOARD FOR 'ASK AND TELL' GAME

36 ask	37 ask	38 tell	39 ask	40 tell	41 tell	42 ask	END
35 tell							
34 ask	33 tell	32 ask	31 tell	30 tell	29 ask	28 tell	27 ask
							26 tell
18 tell	19 ask	20 tell	21 tell	22 tell	23 ask	24 tell	25 ask
17 ask							
16 ask	15 ask	14 tell	13 ask	12 tell	11 ask	10 tell	9 tell
							8 ask
START	1 ask	2 tell	3 ask	4 tell	5 ask	6 ask	7 tell

ASK AND TELL GAME ('ask' cards)

ask cards	**Ask someone:** why he/she wants to learn English.	**Ask someone:** what sort of things he/she is afraid of.	**Ask someone:** which person from history he/she hates most.	**Ask someone:** if there is something he/she would like to buy one day.	**Ask someone:** what sort of things make him/her happy.
Ask someone: to say something about the main political parties in his/her country.	**Ask someone:** what he/she usually does in the evenings.	**Ask someone:** what sort of things make him/her laugh.	**Ask someone:** to tell you about a dream he/she remembers.	**Ask someone:** about any pets he/she has (or used to have).	**Ask someone:** to tell you about the most exciting thing that has ever happened to him/her.
Ask someone: about his/her favourite country for a holiday (and why).	**Ask someone:** if he/she is like his/her mother or father.	**Ask someone:** to tell you about the last book he/she read.	**Ask someone:** about his/her idea of the perfect teacher, husband or wife.	**Ask someone:** how he/she usually spends his/her free time.	**Ask someone:** about the place where he/she lives.
Ask someone: where he/she was born and what he/she remembers most from his/her childhood.	**Ask someone:** to describe his/her living-room.	**Ask someone:** how many new English words he/she hopes to learn on this course.	**Ask someone:** about his/her favourite sport.	**Ask someone:** to tell you two or three things he/she is not very good at.	**Ask someone:** what thing about himself/herself he/she would like to change.
Ask someone: what he/she is going to do at the weekend.	**Ask someone:** about his/her favourite restaurant.	**Ask someone:** what he/she remembers about his/her first or last day at school.	**Ask someone:** if he/she has ever been in a situation that was dangerous or frightening.	**Ask someone:** about his/her plans for the summer.	**Ask someone:** which person from history he/she would most like to have met (and why).
Ask someone: what he/she thinks is the ideal age to get married.	**Ask someone:** about the type of job he/she would like to have.	**Ask someone:** about a country he/she would like to visit (and why).	**Ask someone:** to describe a good TV programme he/she has seen recently.	**Ask someone:** what sort of films he/she likes watching.	**Ask someone:** his/her idea of a well-dressed man and woman.

75 ASK AND TELL GAME ('tell' cards)

tell cards	Tell the others: about someone you were really friendly with at school.	Tell the others: something about the town or village where you were born.	Tell the others: anything you can remember about the first boy/girl you were attracted to.	Tell the others: about some of the things that make you angry or annoyed.	Tell the others: why your country would be a good place to visit as a tourist.
Tell the others: about the types of clothes you like and don't like wearing.	Tell the others: something about the flat/house where you live.	Tell the others: about your last visit abroad.	Tell the others: about any other places you have lived.	Tell the others: one or two things you are quite good at.	Tell the others: which person (still alive!) you would most like to meet and why.
Tell the others: about the nicest present you have ever received.	Tell the others: something about your favourite relative.	Tell the others: about the type of music you like and dislike.	Tell the others: where you hope to go on holiday in the summer.	Tell the others: about a teacher at school you looked up to.	Tell the others: about your childhood.
Tell the others: what you like doing in your free time.	Tell the others: about any incident that made you feel embarrassed or ashamed.	Tell the others: about the type of men/women you are attracted to.	Tell the others: about a country you would not like to visit and why.	Tell the others: something about one of your brothers, sisters or friends.	Tell the others: about a good film you have seen recently.
Tell the others: about a book you would recommend that they all read.	Tell the others: where you usually go to buy clothes.	Tell the others: about someone who has made a big impression on you.	Tell the others: what things you find difficult to learn in English.	Tell the others: what things from your country you would miss if you ever emigrated.	Tell the others: about your favourite dish (and how to cook it!)
Tell the others: where you used to go and what you used to do when you were a teenager.	Tell the others: two good points and two bad points about yourself.	Tell the others: what you are planning to do after this lesson.	Tell the others: where you spent last weekend.	Tell the others: which jobs you think carry the most prestige in your country.	Tell the others: a good way of learning new words in English.

complain	about	think	about	against
the law	insure	against	surprised	at
at	a distance	at	home	at
the age of	by	accident	by	train
arrest	for	die	for	feel sorry
for	famous	for	for	example
hope	for	wait	for	absent
from	escape	from	recover	from
believe	in	in	advance	in
love	translate	into	divide	into
ashamed	of	dream	of	keen
on	on	holiday	insist	on
on	fire	allergic	to	belong
to	look forward	to	angry	with
pleasure	popular	with	disagree	with

For a person you loved deeply, would you be willing to move to a distant country knowing there would be little chance of ever seeing your family and friends again?	If you knew there would be a nuclear war in one week, what would you do?	Would you have one of your fingers surgically removed if it somehow guaranteed immunity from all major diseases?	Would you like to know the precise date of your death?
You discover your wonderful 2-year-old daughter is, because of a mix-up at the hospital, not yours. Would you want to exchange the child to try to correct the mistake?	Would you accept twenty-five years of extraordinary happiness if it meant you would die at the end of the period?	Would you accept a job twice as good as your present one – twice as much money and twice as fulfilling – given one condition of employment; you can never reveal anything about it to anyone you know?	In a nice restaurant, after getting the bill for an excellent meal, you notice that you were not charged for one of the items you ate. Would you tell the waitress?
You are given the power to kill people. They would die a natural death and no one would suspect you. Are there any situations in which you would use this power?	Your house, containing everything you own, catches fire. After saving your loved ones and pets, you have time to safely make a final dash to save any one item. What would it be?	If you were having difficulty on an important test and could safely cheat by looking at someone else's paper, would you do so?	If you could prevent either an earthquake that would kill 40,000 people, a plane crash that would kill 200 people, or a car accident that would kill a friend of yours, which would you choose?
Would you rather be extremely successful professionally and have a fairly ordinary private life, or have a very happy private life and only an ordinary professional life?	Before you are ten pistols – only one of which is loaded. For £1 million would you pick one up, point it at your forehead and press the trigger? If you survive, you keep the money.	If you could take a one-month trip anywhere in the world and money were not a consideration, where would you go and what would you do?	If you could script the basic plot for the dream you will have tonight, what would the story be?
Would you be willing to become extremely ugly physically if it meant you would live for 500 years at any physical age you chose?	Someone close to you is in pain, paralysed and will die within a month. He begs you to give him poison so that he can die. Would you? What if it were your father?	Would you be willing to reduce your life expectancy by five years to become extremely attractive?	Assuming that you had no children and felt the only way for you to have a family was to marry someone you didn't love, would you be willing to do so?
Would you be willing to murder an innocent person if it would end hunger in the world?	For £20,000 would you go for three months without washing, brushing your teeth, or using a deodorant? Assume you could not explain your reasons to anyone.	Given the ability to project yourself into the past but not return, would you do so? Where would you go and what would you try to accomplish if you knew you might change the course of history?	If a crystal ball would tell you the truth about any one thing you wished to know concerning yourself, life, the future, or anything else, what would you want to know?

COUNTABLE	UNCOUNTABLE
apple	air
banana	bread
biscuit	butter
bottle	cheese
car	gold
child	ice
egg	milk
flower	money
hat	music
house	rice
newspaper	salt
onion	soup
orange	sugar
potato	tea
sausage	tennis
umbrella	water

COUNTABLE	UNCOUNTABLE
animal	advice
briefcase	behaviour
brochure	equipment
camera	excitement
city	furniture
coin	homework
competition	information
country	knowledge
family	luggage
impression	news
job	permission
key	scenery
opinion	traffic
sofa	travel
suggestion	weather
war	work

80 COMPLETE THE STORY 1

These are the missing verbs from the story.

became	gave	make	reached
caught	got	make sure	set out
could	had finished	met	slept
decided	had left	misread	understand
drove	hitchhiking	missed	welcomed
explained	know	persuade	were sent
found	lost	put	woke up

Gaps:

1 _____

2 _____

3 _____

4 _____

5 _____

6 _____

7 _____

8 _____

9 _____

10 _____

11 _____

12 _____

13 _____

14 _____

15 _____

16 _____

17 _____

18 _____

19 _____

20 _____

21 _____

22 _____

23 _____

24 _____

25 _____

26 _____

27 _____

28 _____

Read out the following story, leaving gaps for the students to fill in.

The Longest Day

This story happened a few years ago when British people could go on a day trip to France without a passport. It is about a Mr and Mrs Elham who went on a day trip to Boulogne.

When they *(1...had finished...)* their shopping, the couple *(2...set out...)* for a stroll to see the sights of the town. Unfortunately, they didn't *(3...know...)* much French and couldn't really *(4...understand...)* the street signs, so they *(5...became...)* completely lost. The French people they *(6...met...)* were very kind and eventually they *(7...got...)* a lift to the railway station.

As the last ferry *(8...had left...)*, the Elhams *(9...decided...)* to go to Paris and *(10...make...)* their way back to Dover from there. Unfortunately, they *(11...caught...)* the wrong train and *(12...found...)* themselves the next morning – in Luxembourg! The local police *(13...put...)* the confused passengers on a train for Paris and they *(14...slept...)* most of the way – all too soundly in fact, for they *(15...missed...)* their connection and *(16...woke up...)* in Basel in Switzerland!

The obliging Swiss police *(17...gave...)* the couple directions back to Boulogne but somehow they *(18...lost...)* their way again and ended up *(19...hitchhiking...)* over sixty kilometres to Vesoul in central France. A long-distance lorry driver gave the confused couple a lift to Paris, but when they *(20...reached...)* the Gare du Nord, their troubles were not over.

'We *(21...misread...)* the signs,' Mrs Elham *(22...explained...)*, 'and took the train to Bonn in Germany.'

From Germany the Elhams *(23...were sent...)* quickly back to France. At the border, a sympathetic gendarme decided to *(24...make sure...)* they got to Boulogne safely, so he *(25...drove...)* them all the way there.

As they didn't have passports, it took twenty-four hours to *(26...persuade...)* the Customs that their unlikely tale *(27...could...)* possibly be true. But at last they were allowed on a ferry and soon the familiar white cliffs of Dover *(28...welcomed...)* the Elhams back to England.

81 COMPLETE THE STORY 2

quarrelling	grew tired	how	each	from
into	was done	because	in the end	shouted
break	easily	against	no matter	be done
should be	although	remained	show	untied
handed	were told	shrugged	loudly	patiently
be broken	understand	had been trying	themselves	fall
discussing	grew old	what	both	between
for	were done	in spite of	in the beginning	whispered
shake	hardly	upon	despite	be made
can be	even if	was remaining	indicate	tied up
shared	was told	has shrugged	lovingly	bravely
be dropped	understood	is trying	themself	sit

Read out the following story, leaving gaps.

A man and his sons

Once there was a man who had five sons. Instead of living together calmly and quietly, these sons were always *(...quarrelling...)* among themselves.

Their father *(...grew tired...)* of their constant quarrelling. He made up his mind to show them *(...how...)* silly they were.

He picked five sticks, *(...each...)* the same length, *(...from...)* the woodpile. Then he tied them together *(...into...)* a bundle. When this *(...was done...)*, he called his five sons to him. At first they did not hear him *(...because...)* they were too busy arguing, but *(...in the end...)* they came.

'Listen to me!' *(...shouted...)* their father. 'Take this bundle of sticks and *(...break...)* it over your knee.'

'I can do that *(...easily...)*,' said the eldest son.

He took the bundle and pulled it *(...against...)* his knee with all his force. *(...No matter...)* how hard he tried, he could not break the five sticks in the bundle.

'It can't *(...be done...)*,' he growled at last.

'Of course it can,' shouted his brothers. They all began arguing as to which of them *(...should be...)* the one to break the bundle. In the end they all tried in turn. *(...Although...)* their knees became sore, the bundle of sticks *(...remained...)* unbroken.

'Now let me *(...show...)* you how it can be done,' said their father.

He took the bundle of sticks from the others and *(...untied...)* the rope which held them together. Then he *(...handed...)* one stick to each of his five sons.

'Now, each of you break the stick in your hands,' he ordered.

The sons did as they *(...were told...)*. Each stick cracked easily, like pieces of matchwood.

'What do you make of that?' their father asked them.

His sons looked puzzled. They *(...shrugged...)* their shoulders and made no answer. Their father sighed *(...loudly...)*.

'Don't you see?' he explained *(...patiently...)*. 'When a man stands alone, he can *(...be broken...)* as easily as one of those sticks. But when a man stands united with others nothing can break him.'

Only then did his sons *(...understand...)* what their father *(...had been trying...)* to tell them, and they were all ashamed of *(...themselves...)*.

And the moral of the story is: United we stand, divided we *(...fall...)*.

run	see	talk	meet
look at	shout	buy	drink
laugh	drive	kiss	travel
dog	book	restaurant	doctor
beard	plumber	apples	station
tennis	police	money	France
June	birthday	cakes	student
hungry	jealous	kind	happy
strong	tired	modern	red
empty	old	ill	wet
quietly	slowly	politely	angrily
at first	in the end	under the table	through the park
in March	yesterday	last week	in 1994

83 MAKING COMPARISONS/FINDING SIMILARITIES AND DIFFERENCES

Here are the sets of words to use for making comparisons and finding similarities and differences.

Set 1
drums – flute – guitar – piano – trumpet – violin

Set 2
bull – cat – lion – mouse – snake – spider

Set 3
bed – bookcase – carpet – sofa – stool – table

Set 4
bread – chocolate – cream cakes – curry – fruit – spaghetti

Set 5
aeroplane – boat – bus – car – motorbike – taxi

Set 6
boots – dress – hat – jeans – suit – tie

Set 7
baker – dentist – estate agent – nurse – politician – taxi driver

Set 8
café – cinema – hotel – restaurant – school – station

Set 9
dancing – gardening – golf – knitting – stamp collecting – tennis

Set 10
Australia – Brazil – China – Japan – Scotland – Spain

84 GIVE AN ANSWER 1

Write your answers here. Remember, each answer must begin with 'Yes' or 'No'.

1 _____

2 _____

3 _____

4 _____

5 _____

6 _____

7 _____

8 _____

9 _____

10 _____

85 GIVE AN ANSWER 2

Write your answers here.

1 _____

2 _____

3 _____

4 _____

5 _____

6 _____

7 _____

8 _____

9 _____

10 _____

11 _____

12 _____

84 GIVE AN ANSWER 1 (Teacher's sheet)

Read out the following, pausing after each one to allow the students to write down their answers.

1 Number 1. Is Paul a teacher?

2 Number 2. Do you smoke?

3 Number 3. Was it cold yesterday?

4 Number 4. Does your mother drive?

5 Number 5. Were you born in Greece?

6 Number 6. Is she hungry?

7 Number 7. Are your parents interested in pop music?

8 Number 8. Do you usually go abroad in the summer?

9 Number 9. Can you speak German?

10 Number 10. Are you married?

- -

85 GIVE AN ANSWER 2 (Teacher's sheet)

Read out the following, pausing after each one to allow the students to write down their answers.

1 Number 1. You've put on weight.

2 Number 2. The window's broken!

3 Number 3. Carol looks happy.

4 Number 4. Peter's in a really bad mood today.

5 Number 5. You forgot to phone me!

6 Number 6. Pam and Dave aren't talking to each other.

7 Number 7. Your hands are dirty!

8 Number 8. It's freezing in here!

9 Number 9. You still haven't paid me back the £20 you owe me!

10 Number 10. My car won't start.

11 Number 11. You're late again!

12 Number 12. Janet's lost her voice.

Look at this drawing for five minutes. You are not allowed to write anything down.

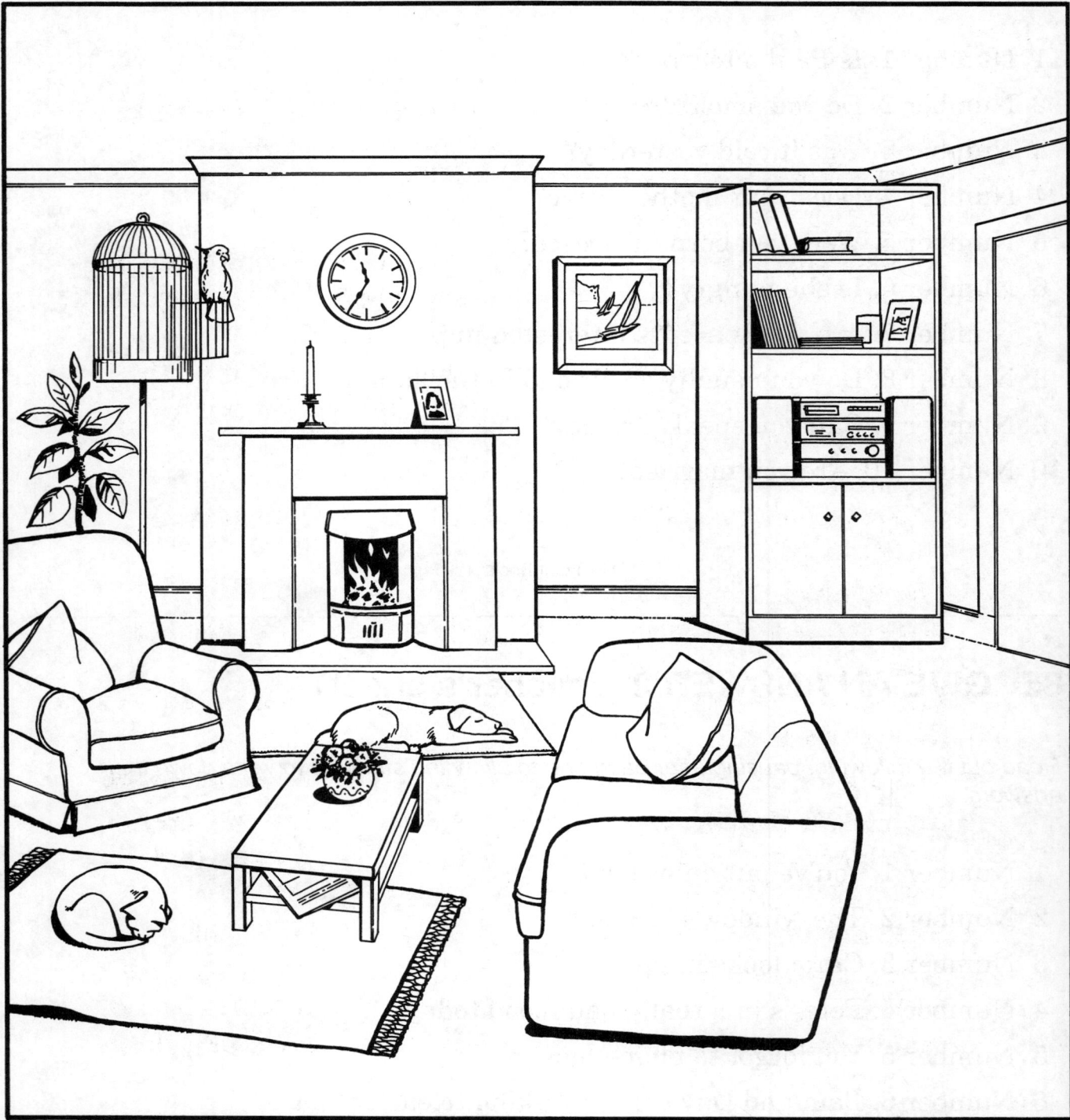

When your teacher tells you to stop, turn your drawing over, then write down the answers to the questions you will be asked on a separate piece of paper. Number them 1–15.

The following facts are all completely untrue, but are often thought to be true or have appeared in newspapers as true stories. They are known as urban myths. Read through them for five minutes. You are not allowed to write anything down.

- If a large vicious dog attacks you, the best way to avoid being badly bitten is to grab its front legs and quickly pull them apart sideways, killing the dog instantly.

- If you pick a hamster up by the tail, its eyes pop out.

- A woman once lost her watch on a Devon beach. Years later, her husband caught a fish in the same spot and it had her watch inside – still keeping perfect time.

- Scientists have invented a car that runs on water, but all the world's oil companies have got together, paid off the scientists involved, and are keeping the invention secret.

- It is quite common for dead passengers to travel around undisturbed for days on the Tokyo metro – even sometimes standing up.

- The Bank of England has to buy every new model of photocopier, fax or laser printer to see how well they can forge notes.

- You can fully recharge phone cards by putting them in the freezer overnight.

- The ink for US dollar bills comes from crushed butterfly wings.

- An ancient British law, still valid but little used, states that if you stop someone in the street and can correctly guess how much money they have in their pocket, you can keep it.

- Shop mirrors are trick ones that make you look slimmer.

- There's a special number you can dial on your telephone that will make all your calls free from then on. When people are caught doing it, they're charged with another crime and it's all hushed up.

- Dozens of commuters on London Underground kill themselves every year by falling asleep. Apparently, they wake up confused and accidentally walk out of the train door between stations.

When your teacher tells you to stop, turn your paper over. You are now going to be tested. Write your answers on a separate piece of paper. Number them 1–12.

153

86   THE MEMORY GAME 1 (Teacher's sheet)

Read out the following. Pause between each question to allow the students time to write down their answers.

1 What time was it?
2 How many cushions were there altogether?
3 There was a painting on the wall. Was it of a person? If not, what was the motif?
4 Was there a television set in the bookcase? If so, on which shelf was it?
5 Was there anything on the mantelpiece? If so, what?
6 How many armchairs were there?
7 Was there a rug in front of the fire?
8 What was on the coffee table? And under it?
9 Was the plant next to or behind the armchair?
10 Was the fire alight?
11 Was the door open or closed?
12 Were there more than ten books on the top shelf of the bookcase?
13 What was on the bottom shelf of the bookcase?
14 Name any animals in the room.
15 Was there a standard lamp behind the sofa?

87   THE MEMORY GAME 2 (Teacher's sheet)

Read out the following. Pause between each question to allow the students time to write down their answers.

1 What happens if you dial a special, secret telephone number?
2 Why is it dangerous to fall asleep on the London Underground?
3 Why do the Bank of England test all new photocopiers, faxes and laser printers?
4 What had the woman lost? Who found it and where?
5 Where might you find ink made from crushed butterfly wings?
6 If a vicious dog attacks you, how can you protect yourself?
7 What, according to an ancient British law, can you do to legally get another person's money?
8 How can you recharge phone cards?
9 What happens to a hamster if you pick it up by its tail?
10 What sometimes happens on the Tokyo metro?
11 Why have the oil companies paid off some scientists?
12 What's so special about shop mirrors?

88 WHAT DOES IT MEAN?

Listen and write the numbers 1–16 next to the correct sentences.

a 'Don't let on!' _____

b 'He's always looked down on foreigners.' _____

c 'I can put you up.' _____

d 'I really must cut down.' _____

e 'I think it's going to clear up.' _____

f 'I'll call on you tonight.' _____

g 'I'm getting on a bit now.' _____

h 'I'm worn out.' _____

i 'I've been beaten up.' _____

j 'It keeps breaking down.' _____

k 'It's been held up.' _____

l 'She's passed out.' _____

m 'They've decided to take me on.' _____

n 'We had to have him put down.' _____

o 'We turn out about a thousand a day.' _____

p 'We've fallen out again.' _____

Read out the sentences in this order:

1 Write the number 1 next to the person who has been attacked.
   (i   I've been beaten up.)

2 Write the number 2 next to the person who has just been given a job. *(m   They've decided to take me on.)*

3 Write the number 3 next to the person who has quarrelled with someone. *(p   We've fallen out again.)*

4 Write the number 4 next to the person who wants something to be kept a secret. *(a   Don't let on!)*

5 Write the number 5 next to the person who is really tired.
   (h   I'm worn out.)

6 Write the number 6 next to the person who might be talking about a pet that has died. *(n   We had to have him put down.)*

7 Write the number 7 next to the person who is offering someone a room for the night. *(c   I can put you up.)*

8 Write the number 8 next to the person who might be talking about the goods produced at a factory.
   (o   We turn out about a thousand a day.)

9 Write the number 9 next to the person who is talking about a racist.
   (b   He's always looked down on foreigners.)

10 Write the number 10 next to the person who might be talking about a bus or a train that is late. *(k   It's been held up.)*

11 Write the number 11 next to the person who might be worried about the number of cigarettes he or she smokes.
   (d   I really must cut down.)

12 Write the number 12 next to the person who is talking about someone who has fainted. *(l   She's passed out.)*

13 Write the number 13 next to the person who is talking about his or her age. *(g   I'm getting on a bit now.)*

14 Write the number 14 next to the person who is talking about the weather. *(e   I think it's going to clear up.)*

15 Write the number 15 next to the person who is talking about visiting someone. *(f   I'll call on you tonight.)*

16 Write the number 16 next to the person who probably wishes he or she had a better car. *(j   It keeps breaking down.)*

89 EXPLAIN YOURSELF!

You were climbing through your neighbour's upstairs window.
You took your cousin's dog for a walk and came back with a completely different one.
You were running through the park dressed as a gorilla.
You were driving your car on the wrong side of the road.
You were chasing a policeman down the street.
You were sitting on the roof of the school crying.
You came to school with your face and arms painted blue.
You were at a disco dressed as a member of the opposite sex.
You were washing your clothes in the local river.
You were throwing stones angrily at a large Coca-Cola sign.
You were pushing your teacher down the road in a pram.
You were standing on your head outside the cinema eating a banana.
You stood up and started singing loudly in the middle of your English exam.

90 COMPLETE THE SENTENCES 1

Work alone. Complete the following sentences in your own words.

1 When I have some free time I like to _____.

2 I find it very easy to _____.

3 My least favourite animals are _____.

4 I would describe myself as _____ and_____.
   (use two adjectives)

5 The first thing I do when I wake up in the morning is _____
   _____.

6 Learning English is easy/hard *(choose)* because_____
   _____.

7 I want to _____ before I'm 50.

8 I enjoy eating _____ and _____. *(name two dishes)*

9 It is better to be a man/woman *(choose)* because men/women _____
   _____.

10 I'm learning English because_____.

11 I hate people who _____.

12 Middle age starts at the age of _____.

13 I don't like films which _____.

14 I like going to parties where _____.

15 _____ makes me nervous/cry/laugh. *(choose)*

16 A friend is someone _____.

When you have finished, work with 2–3 others. Talk about and compare your answers.

91 COMPLETE THE SENTENCES 2

Work alone. Complete the following sentences in your own words.

1 The happiest/saddest/funniest *(choose)* memory I have from school is

   _____ .

2 As a child I used to spend my summer holidays _____ .

3 The best film I have ever seen is _____ .

4 One day I hope to _____ .

5 I've always wanted to _____ .

6 I'd love to visit _____ .

7 The part of my body I'd like to change most is _____ .

8 The most beautiful place I have ever visited is _____ .

9 The most frightening thing I ever experienced was _____

   _____ .

10 I would find it very difficult to live without _____ and

   _____ .*(name two things, not people)*

11 _____ and _____ are two of the most useful things
   ever invented.

12 When we used to misbehave in class, our teachers would _____

   _____ .

13 Next year I'm going to _____ .

14 Every married couple should _____ .

15 _____ and _____are two things I've never tried
   doing.

16 I once got into trouble at school/home *(choose)* for _____ .

17 The last time I laughed/cried *(choose)* a lot was _____ .

18 The best birthday present anyone could give me would be _____ .

When you have finished, work with 2–3 others. Talk about and compare your answers.

92 COMPLETE THE SENTENCES 3

Work alone. Complete the following sentences in your own words.

1 I'm not very interested _____.

2 In school I was always very good _____, but pretty bad
_____.

3 When I visited _____ *(name a country)*, I was very
impressed _____.

4 I am sometimes envious _____.

5 My mother/father/brother/sister/friend *(choose)* is very proud _____
_____.

6 The first/last *(choose)* job I applied _____.

7 I am/am not *(choose)* easily shocked _____.

8 Compared _____ *(say a nationality)*, people in my country
_____.

9 As a child I used to be afraid _____.

10 I would hate to die _____.

11 When I'm feeling depressed I always _____.

12 When I go out with friends, we usually _____.

13 Teachers should never _____.

14 When I go abroad I nearly always _____.

15 When I'm short of money, I sometimes _____.

16 I don't often go _____ or play _____.

17 For a change at weekends I sometimes _____.

18 Only once in my life have I _____.

19 I could never_____, even if someone offered me
£1 million.

20 When I want to enjoy myself I usually _____.

When you have finished, work with 2-3 others. Talk about and compare your answers.

93 COMPLETE THE SENTENCES 4

Work alone. Complete the following sentences in your own words.

1 If I won a lot of money _____.

2 If I decide to go out this weekend, I'll probably _____.

3 Most people would be a lot happier if _____.

4 If men had babies instead of women _____.

5 If I could have any job in the world _____.

6 If I go abroad in the summer, I _____.

7 If I could meet someone famous _____.

8 If you want to make a good impression at an interview you should
_____.

9 If someone pays me a compliment I usually_____.

10 I wish I'd never _____.

11 If I could be another nationality _____.

12 If a friend of mine got into trouble _____.

13 Children would work a lot harder at school if _____.

14 If my car was stolen _____.

15 English would be an easier language to learn if _____
_____.

16 If I could change one thing about my life at present _____
_____.

17 Most parents would be very unhappy/pleased/worried/excited *(choose)*
if their children _____.

18 If I could have my life again, I definitely wouldn't _____.

19 If I ever emigrated _____.

20 If you asked me to cook you a meal, I'd make _____.

When you have finished, work with 2–3 others. Talk about and compare your answers.

94   RIGHT WORD, WRONG PLACE 1

Work in pairs. In each of the sentences below underline the two words which should change places with each other in order to make sense.

Example: The <u>cinema</u> went to the <u>children</u>

1 He put his pocket in his wallet.
2 She lives the near park.
3 The room was warm, so they lit a cold fire.
4 You must quiet be in the library.
5 Take an umbrella it case in rains.
6 Thirty eight and twelve make forty six.
7 If yesterday was Friday then tomorrow is Wednesday.
8 Every work I go to day.
9 He tennis to play likes.
10 She never vegetables eats.
11 All child ate the the biscuits.
12 Piano likes to play the she.
13 Her tennis sport is favourite.
14 Our roof has a blue house.
15 I have films all those seen.
16 She to likes listen to pop music.
17 the wide is very river here.
18 I think exciting is flying.
19 Today is raining it.
20 I usually to go bed early.

95   RIGHT WORD, WRONG PLACE 2

Work in pairs. In each of the sentences below underline the two words which should change places with each other in order to make sense.

Example   The <u>park</u> played in the <u>children</u>.

1 The the bit dog postman.
2 I fast my car drive.
3 This time we week next will be in Paris.
4 James was unable, so was ill to go to the party.
5 Was the party everyone after very tired.
6 Park fed the ducks in the they.
7 Put which cupboard shall I into the cups?
8 I French learning to speak am.
9 The plane landing as it was crashed.
10 She is interested at music and that's why she's so good in it.
11 There is a bank near here?
12 Grass off the keep!
13 He hopes to when a doctor become he leaves school.
14 I hair to cut my need soon.
15 She is getting married on 6 o'clock at Friday.
16 You can like what you say about him, I still don't think he's a very good actor.
17 We'll have a picnic it long as as doesn't rain.
18 Take an case with you in umbrella it rains.
19 Please put those drawers in the forks.
20 I'm sorry I've waiting you kept.
21 He couldn't hoarse because his voice was speak.
22 Like you do watching television?
23 Is a there post office near here?
24 Its a well-known fact that a racing pigeon can usually find it's way home.
25 She got into of her car and went out the house.

You must bet between 10 and 100 points for each statement.

Statement	Right	Wrong	Bet	Loss	Gain
1 This food smells nice. What is it?	❑	❑	_____	_____	_____
2 One of my hobbies are photography.	❑	❑	_____	_____	_____
3 She went to the hairdresser to have her hairs cut.	❑	❑	_____	_____	_____
4 She is born in France.	❑	❑	_____	_____	_____
5 'What's Sally doing?' 'She's having a shower.'	❑	❑	_____	_____	_____
6 How long has your sister been married?	❑	❑	_____	_____	_____
7 She speaks English very good.	❑	❑	_____	_____	_____
8 That building over there is the most tall building in London.	❑	❑	_____	_____	_____
9 She's very pretty, isn't she?	❑	❑	_____	_____	_____
10 There is two cats in the garden.	❑	❑	_____	_____	_____
11 Everyone in this class comes from Germany.	❑	❑	_____	_____	_____
12 Can I lend your pen, please?	❑	❑	_____	_____	_____
13 He goes to the cinema a lot but hardly ever to the theatre.	❑	❑	_____	_____	_____
14 He like watching television very much.	❑	❑	_____	_____	_____
15 How many money have you got?	❑	❑	_____	_____	_____

Total losses/gains: _____ _____

GRAND TOTAL: ⬭
(Gains minus losses)

You must bet between 10 and 100 points for each statement.

Statement	Right	Wrong	Bet	Loss	Gain
1 I'd like an information about trains to London.	❏	❏	___	___	___
2 Paul is here for two weeks. He goes back at the end of the month.	❏	❏	___	___	___
3 She was having a bath when the phone rang.	❏	❏	___	___	___
4 I haven't seen her since three days.	❏	❏	___	___	___
5 I'm not very good in tennis.	❏	❏	___	___	___
6 There isn't much furniture in my flat.	❏	❏	___	___	___
7 I'll have an ice-cream. Will you have some too?	❏	❏	___	___	___
8 Are you sure you can carry it? It's rather heavy.	❏	❏	___	___	___
9 'It looks like rain.' 'Oh, I don't hope so.'	❏	❏	___	___	___
10 We won't go to the beach unless it stops raining.	❏	❏	___	___	___
11 I am living in Hastings for five years.	❏	❏	___	___	___
12 This is the third time he is arriving home late this week.	❏	❏	___	___	___
13 I want some apples. Have you got any?	❏	❏	___	___	___
14 What an awful news!	❏	❏	___	___	___
15 Please remember me to post these letters, will you?	❏	❏	___	___	___

Total losses/gains: _____ _____

GRAND TOTAL:
(Gains minus losses)

You must bet between 10 and 100 points for each statement.

Statement	Right	Wrong	Bet	Loss	Gain
1 I look forward to seeing you next week.	❑	❑	_____	_____	_____
2 By this time next week we'll be in the south of France.	❑	❑	_____	_____	_____
3 He didn't finish doing his homework yet.	❑	❑	_____	_____	_____
4 Jane's mother, whose seventy, plays tennis regularly.	❑	❑	_____	_____	_____
5 We had so nice weather last week. It was really hot.	❑	❑	_____	_____	_____
6 She had always regarded him as her friend.	❑	❑	_____	_____	_____
7 You will pass your exam if you will work hard.	❑	❑	_____	_____	_____
8 Is there anything more you'd like me to get you?	❑	❑	_____	_____	_____
9 If you should see John, tell him I'll phone him tomorrow night.	❑	❑	_____	_____	_____
10 The weather is less colder today than it was yesterday.	❑	❑	_____	_____	_____
11 They looked loving at each other.	❑	❑	_____	_____	_____
12 If I were you I'd sell now. You're not likely to get a better offer.	❑	❑	_____	_____	_____
13 One of the nicest parks in London is the Hyde Park.	❑	❑	_____	_____	_____
14 You'll phone as soon as you get there, won't you?	❑	❑	_____	_____	_____
15 'Cardiff is in Wales, isn't it?' 'Yes, I believe so.'	❑	❑	_____	_____	_____

Total losses/gains: _____   _____

GRAND TOTAL: ⬭
(Gains minus losses)

99   A LIFE HISTORY

Work in pairs or groups of three. Read the following:

Name: Peter Redman

Age: 42

Nationality: British

Family details:
Father: musician
Mother: teacher
2 brothers, 1 sister
Married. 1 child

Brief life history

Peter was born in Liverpool. He left school at 16 and got a job at a local garage. He didn't like this very much so, at the age of 18, he moved to London. There he got a job at a West End theatre. While working there he wrote a play. He showed it to one of the actors who liked it so much that he persuaded a director friend of his to put it on. It was a huge success. After that Peter wrote three more plays – all of them equally successful.

In 1980 he was invited to Hollywood to write the screenplay of one of his first plays. The film was a big hit and he won an Oscar for his screenplay. He decided to move to America to write more screenplays. While there he met and fell in love with the actress Dawn Fairchild. They got married in 1985 and moved to New York. Two years later, their daughter, Katie, was born. While in New York, Peter wrote his first novel which became an international best-seller.

Peter and Dawn are now planning to move back to Britain, possibly somewhere near Liverpool.

Interests and hobbies

Windsurfing, golf and painting. Has also started to learn to fly a helicopter and hopes to buy his own helicopter when the family moves back to Britain.

Now try to make up your own life history for one of the people in the photographs you will get from your teacher. Try to lay it out in the same way as above, using the following headings:

Name, Age, Nationality, Family details, Brief life history and Interests and hobbies.

100 LOOKING AFTER FOREIGN VISITORS

Work in pairs or groups of three. Imagine you have invited some English friends of yours to spend a week in your country some time during the summer. This is the first time they will have visited your country, so you want to give them a good time and to show them as much as possible.

Discuss and decide what you will do with your friends. Talk about:

• the best time to come to your country
• where you will go
• what you will see
• what you will do
• what souvenirs to take home with them
etc.

Write your daily plans here.

	morning	afternoon	evening
Day 1	Arrive 10.25.		
Day 2			
Day 3			
Day 4			
Day 5			
Day 6			
Day 7	Depart 11.20.		

When you have finished, work with another group. Take it in turns to talk about the plans you have made.

101 WHAT'S THE QUESTION? 1

Look at the following examples.

I'm listening to **the radio**.
She wants to dance with **you**.
We're going to **the cinema** tonight

What are you listening to?
Who does she want to dance with?
Where are you going tonight?

*Now write questions to the following answers. Remember your question must be based on the words in **bold type**.*

1 You can start work **on Monday**. _____

2 **The last exercise** was the hardest. _____

3 He met his wife **at a party**. _____

4 Margaret weighs **65 kilos**. _____

5 We have seen the film **three times**. _____

6 He bought **three new shirts**. _____

7 She paid **by cheque**. _____

8 The car cost **£5,000**. _____

9 There were **more than 10,000 people** at the pop concert. _____

10 He sees his parents **twice a week**. _____

11 They are staying with **their cousin**. _____

12 **Janet** doesn't like spaghetti. _____

13 We had to wait **over half an hour** for our train. _____

14 Cathy lives **in Chelsea**. _____

15 She's got a flat **on the third floor**. _____

16 They have gone to France **for two weeks**. _____

17 Hastings is **about 60 miles** from London. _____

18 Cathy has worked here **since 1987**. _____

19 She is upset **because she wasn't invited to the party**. _____

20 **John's** wife is called Mandy. _____

Work in pairs or groups of three. Read the following extract from a newspaper.

Countdown to catastrophe

THIS is the sequence of events leading to the assassination of President Kennedy on November 22, 1963, and the subsequent death of his alleged assassin, Lee Harvey Oswald.

7.15 am: Oswald is spotted carrying a long object, wrapped in paper, when he arrives for work at the Texas School Book Depository in Dallas.

9.30 am-10.30 am: He is seen staring out of a first-floor window which overlooks Dealey Plaza.

11.40 am: A worker at the depository notices Oswald looking out of the window on the sixth floor from where the shots are fired.

12.30 pm: The motorcade turns in to Elm Street directly in front of the depository and shots ring out. In the confusion, Oswald slips out of the building.

12.45 pm: Dallas police issue a description: unknown white male, approximately 30, slender build, height 5ft 10in.

1.15 pm: Patrolman J.D. Tippit sees Oswald on East Street. He pulls over and calls to Oswald. the patrolman is killed by several shots from Oswald's revolver.

1.46 pm: Police announce: 'Have information a suspect just went into the Texas theatre on West Jefferson.' Within minutes six squad cars arrive and police seal the exits. Theatre lights are turned up and Officer M.N. McDonald confronts Oswald who raises his hands and punches him, saying, 'Well, it's all over now'. Oswald takes out his revolver and pulls the trigger but the gun does not fire. He is overpowered and taken into custody.

November 24: Oswald is gunned down in police custody by Jack Ruby, a nightclub owner who thought his act would make him a national hero.

LEWIS WILLIAMSON

Here are some answers to questions based on the above extract. They are not in any particular order. Write down suitable questions which would give these answers.

1 _____?
Elm Street.

2 _____?
The Texas Theatre.

3 _____?
A nightclub owner.

4 _____?
On November 22, 1963.

5 _____?
No, he didn't.

6 _____?
No, they arrived within minutes.

7 _____?
At 7.15 am.

8 _____?
Because he thought it would make him a national hero.

9 _____?
Between 9.30 am and 10.30 am.

10 _____?
Yes, he was.

11 _____?
A patrolman.

12 _____?
Lee Harvey Oswald.

13 _____?
From the sixth floor.

14 _____?
At the Texas School Book Depository.

15 _____?
No, they were looking for a white man.

What are you afraid of?

		You	Pairs	Group
1	Failing a test or exam.			
2	Looking foolish in front of others.			
3	Being a passenger in an aeroplane.			
4	Rats and mice.			
5	Hyperdermic needles.			
6	Being alone.			
7	Death.			
8	Blood.			
9	Heights.			
10	Losing my job.			
11	Closed spaces, e.g. lifts.			
12	Spiders or snakes.			
13	Strange dogs.			
14	Being alone in a train compartment with a complete stranger.			
15	Thunderstorms.			
16	Meeting someone for the first time.			
17	Speaking in front of a group of people.			
18	Not being a success.			
19	Being a passenger in a car which is being driven fast.			
20	*(Anything else?)*			

What really annoys you?

	You	Pairs	Group

1   A person telling me how to drive.

2   Getting an engaged telephone signal.

3   A person telling me to do something when I'm just about to do it.

4   A person continually criticizing something.

5   Waiting for someone to come to the phone.

6   A person putting his/her hands on me unnecessarily.

7   A person picking his/her teeth.

8   A person with a cold making loud sniffing noises.

9   A person continually trying to be funny.

10   Listening to politicians making promises.

11   Hearing 'loud' music.

12   Being unable to find a seat on a bus or a train.

13   A person watching me work.

14   Hearing racist remarks about immigrants.

15   A person interrupting me when I am speaking.

16   Having a host/hostess repeatedly urging me to take some food I do not want.

17   Seeing colours that clash.

18   Finding a hair in my food.

19   People who jump queues.

20   *(Anything else?)*

What makes a successful marriage?

		You	Pairs	Group
1	Accepting your partner as he/she is.			
2	Having a good relationship with your in-laws.			
3	Having a home of your own. (Not necessarily owning it.)			
4	Being from a similar class and culture.			
5	Both partners being able and willing to cook.			
6	Being able to make each other laugh.			
7	Being able to respect each other's needs.			
8	Having similar interests.			
9	Being faithful to each other.			
10	Being honest.			
11	Both partners being of similar intelligence.			
12	Being able to communicate with each other.			
13	Having similar views, e.g. about politics and religion.			
14	Being willing to work at the marriage.			
15	Being handy about the house.			
16	Having a good physical relationship.			
17	Having good health.			
18	Having children.			

106 CAN IT BE TRUE?

Work in groups of 3–4. Read through the following. Some of the facts are 100% true while others are complete lies. Try to work out which is which.

1 Both Ghandi and Fidel Castro used to be lawyers.

2 The famous Austrian psychoanalyst Sigmund Freud's hobby was mushroom collecting.

3 The actor Dustin Hoffman's real name is David Charles Peschkowsky.

4 The actor Yul Brunner used to be a trapeze artist in a circus. His career ended when he was injured in a fall.

5 The novelist Graham Greene suffered from hematophobia *(fear or blood)* and ornithophobia *(fear of birds)*.

6 If you adjust for inflation, then the film that has made the most money ever is *Star Wars*.

7 The famous novelist Jackie Collins was expelled from Francis Holland School in England for (among other things) truancy and smoking behind a tree during lacrosse.

8 Ex-President Richard Nixon used to be a second-hand car dealer.

9 Woody Allen's son is called Satchel and Frank Zappa's daughter is called Moon Unit.

10 An early name for the Beatles was Johnny and the Moondogs.

11 The actor Tom Cruise, the actor/singer Cher and the politician Nelson Rockefeller all suffered from claustrophobia *(the fear of being shut up in a small, enclosed space, e.g. a lift).*

12 Princess Diana came second in a beauty contest when she was 15.

13 Both Nancy Reagan and Bill Clinton were adopted.

14 The singer Rod Stewart was once a grave digger.

15 Margaret Thatcher was once accidentally arrested for shoplifting.

16 The actor Richard Burton never won an Oscar even though he was nominated for one seven times.

When you have finished, report back to the rest of the class using the following phrases:

It's definitely true that…
It's probably true that…
It might be true that…
It's probably not true that…
It's very unlikely that…
It's definitely not true that…

Read through the following text and fill in the missing prepositions.

RABBIT IN MIXER SURVIVES

A baby rabbit fell _____ a mixing machine _____ a quarry yesterday and came out _____ the middle _____ a concrete block. But the rabbit still had the strength to dig its way free before the block set.

The tiny creature was scooped up _____ 30 tons _____ sand, then swirled and pounded _____ the complete mixing process. Mr Michael Hooper, the machine operator, found the rabbit shivering _____ top _____ the solid concrete block, its coat stiff _____ fragments. A hole _____ the middle _____ the block and paw marks showed the escape route.

Mr Reginald Denslow, the manager _____ the quarry, said: 'This rabbit must have a lot more than nine lives to go _____ this machine. I just don't know how it avoided being suffocated, squashed or cut _____ half.' _____ the 30 tons _____ sand, it was dropped _____ a weighing hopper and carried _____ a conveyor belt to an overhead mixer where it was whirled around _____ gallons _____ water.

_____ there the rabbit was swept _____ a machine which hammers wet concrete _____ blocks _____ a pressure _____ 100 lb per square inch. The rabbit was encased _____ a block 18 inches long, nine inches high and six inches thick. Finally the blocks were ejected _____ to the floor to dry and the dazed rabbit clawed itself free.

'We cleaned him up, dried him _____ the electric fire, then he hopped _____,' Mr Denslaw said.

Now put the following drawings in the right order. Number them 1–10. The first one has been done for you.

108 SORT OUT THE TEXT

The following letter to a newspaper is completely mixed up. See if you can put it in the right order by numbering the lines 1–21. (Some numbers have already been filled in.)

The unexpected visitor

☐ caller was the baker who, if there was no reply, would

☐ footsteps coming slowly across the kitchen towards the

☐ then explained:

☐ and walked out of the house.

1 A friend of mine expecting some visitors to tea at her

☐ downstairs into the kitchen. Her hand was on the

☐ She rushed into the nearest haven: the broom cupboard.

☐ astonished gasman. He had come to read the meter,

☐ The gasman said, 'Oh!' Then he said 'Sorry, mum,' and

☐ country cottage one afternoon this week, popped some

☐ door. She was panic-stricken, for she was sure that her

☐ broom cupboard. The door opened. And there stood an

☐ 'I'm so sorry – I was expecting the baker.'

☐ scones into the oven. An hour later, she was about to

☐ which is in the cupboard. My friend blushed deeply and

☐ Not even stopping to grab a towel, she dashed naked

☐ tipping his cap politely he carefully closed the door again

12 The back door clicked open, and my friend heard

☐ open the door and leave the bread on the kitchen table.

☐ handle of the oven when she heard a knock at the back

☐ step into the bath when she suddenly remembered them.

109 TWENTY QUESTIONS

Work in groups. Put in the missing question words (or preposition plus question words) in the questions below. Then try and answer them. (Your teacher will give you the answers.)

1 _____ would a Roman mathematician have written the number 91?

2 _____ are earthquakes measured?*

3 James Bond has the Secret Service designation 007. _____ is the meaning of 007?

4 _____ Swede invented dynamite in 1866?

5 _____ sport do you associate 'Flushing Meadow'?*

6 _____ of the Great Lakes is Toronto situated?*

7 _____ players are there in a cricket team?

8 _____ were the first men to land on the moon in 1969?

9 _____ did the Vietnam War begin and end?

10 _____ is the Volkswagen car so called?

11 _____ name was Muhammed Ali, the former World Heavyweight Boxing Champion known before he changed it?*

12 _____ novel from 1954 do you meet Ralph, Piggy and Jack Merridew, who are marooned on an uninhabited island after a plane crash?*

13 _____ section of the orchestra does the bassoon belong?*

14 _____ ghost haunted Macbeth in Shakespeare's play of that name?

15 _____ in the world is the range of mountains known as the Southern Alps?

16 _____ is the town of Meissen, in Germany, famous?*

17 _____ country did the first World Cup in football take place?*

18 _____ would you be eating if you were served *Bombay Duck*?

19 _____, according to Conan Doyle, did Sherlock Holmes live?

20 _____ language does the word *tycoon* originate?*

(* Use preposition plus question word.)

Write your answers here.

1 _____   8 _____   15 _____

2 _____   9 _____   16 _____

3 _____   10 _____   17 _____

4 _____   11 _____   18 _____

5 _____   12 _____   19 _____

6 _____   13 _____   20 _____

7 _____   14 _____

110 PLACE THE ADJECTIVES

Rewrite the following sentences putting the adjectives in the correct places and in the correct order.

Example: She was wearing a dress. *(blue, pretty)*
She was wearing a pretty blue dress.

1 We had some soup for lunch. *(hot, delicious)*
_____

2 I'm hot, sweaty and tired. What I could do with now is a bath. *(nice, hot)*
_____

3 She put her groceries in a bag. *(brown, small, plastic)*
_____

4 She had big eyes and a friendly smile. *(blue, warm)*
_____

5 The new boss was a man with about as much charisma as a slug. *(fat, balding, big, middle-aged)*
_____

6 Pam has just bought an evening dress. *(silk, white, long, expensive)*
_____

7 What a man he is! *(pleasant, young, intelligent)*
_____

8 We walked down a street to the harbour. *(cobbled, long, narrow)*
_____

9 Paul was singing a song. *(sentimental, Irish, old)*
_____

10 They're showing a film on TV tonight. *(Western, old, American)*
_____

11 He was very good-looking with dark hair. *(wavy, long, lovely)*
_____

12 Who was that man I saw you with at the party? *(little, boring, dreadful)*
_____

13 It's a sunny day. Let's go to the beach. *(lovely, bright)*
_____

14 He sat down in an armchair. *(leather, comfortable, brown)*
_____

15 I'm looking for a flat. *(cheap, one-roomed, modern)*
_____

16 He used to take sandwiches to work in a box. *(round, metal, small)*
_____

17 She has just bought a sports car. *(Japanese, red, flashy, new)*
_____

18 My brother has just got engaged to a girl. *(blonde, beautiful, Swedish, young)*
_____

19 He was on his way home through the park when he was attacked by a dog. *(black, fierce-looking, big)*
_____

20 The only thing stolen was a watch. *(Swiss, valuable, gold, antique)*
_____

111 PLACE THE ADVERBS

Put the adverbs in the correct places in the following sentences.

1 I visit my parents at the weekend. *(usually)*

2 I watch television, though I listen to the radio. *(hardly ever, frequently)*

3 I don't understand why she didn't come to my party. *(still)*

4 He has had three cars and they have been Volvos. *(all)*

5 I've got two sisters and they're married. *(both)*

6 Have you eaten oysters? *(ever)*

7 I'm going to get married next year. *(probably)*

8 I do wish she'd speak louder. I can hear a word she's saying. *(hardly)*

9 Sue's not very adventurous. She hasn't been abroad. *(even)*

10 My brother-in-law loses his temper. He's so calm and self-controlled. *(hardly ever, always)*

11 I disagree with you. Men are more violent than women. *(completely, definitely)*

12 He goes to bed early but reads for hours before he goes to sleep. *(always, sometimes)*

13 I go jogging these days. There's enough time. *(rarely, never)*

14 My brother plays for the local football team. *(occasionally)*

15 Peter is a good singer and he plays the guitar. *(also)*

16 Cathy has started learning Spanish. *(just)*

17 I haven't finished doing my homework. I've got two more exercises to do. *(yet, still)*

18 You'll pick up French if you spend the whole summer in France. *(certainly)*

19 I saw Jane at the party and I'm going to tell her husband about it. *(definitely)*

20 We get very tired after playing squash. *(always)*

21 Geoff and Ted don't quarrel. *(often)*

22 Pauline Brown? Yes, I saw her yesterday! *(only)*

23 'Is Brian a good student?'
   'Well he works very hard.' *(certainly)*

24 He's got three brothers. They are policemen. *(all)*

25 She plays the piano and comes first in most competitions. *(beautifully, usually)*

What is the most dangerous thing you have ever done?	What is the nicest meal you have ever eaten?
Which is the most interesting country you have ever been to?	What is the closest you have ever been to being seriously injured?
Who are some of the wealthiest people in your country?	Who is the most popular (a) man (b) woman in your country?
Who is the most influential person in history?	What is one of the most expensive things you have ever bought?
When are you happiest?	What is the greatest scientific breakthrough ever?
What is the most you have ever weighed?	What is the fastest you have ever travelled by car?
What is the most frightening thing that has ever happened to you?	Which subjects were you (a) best at (b) worst at when you were at school?
What is the quickest way to (a) lose weight (b) get over a cold?	Who is the most attractive man or woman you have ever seen? (You needn't have met this person.)
Who is the funniest person you know?	What is the best thing that has ever happened to you?
Who is one of the most boring politicians in your country?	Who is the (a) meanest (b) most generous person you have ever met?

What is the most embarrassing thing that has ever happened to you?	Which colour or colours do you (a) look best in (b) look least good in?
What is the (a) most difficult (b) least difficult thing about learning English?	What is the stupidest thing you have ever done?
What is the most popular tourist attraction in your country?	What is the (a) best (b) worst film you have ever seen?
Who is the cleverest person you know personally?	What is the proudest moment of your life so far?
Who is the (a) oldest (b) youngest relative you have?	Who are the worst drivers – men or women?
What is your happiest memory of childhood?	What is the most enjoyable holiday or birthday you have ever had?
What is your least favourite type of (a) music (b) food (c) holiday?	What is the most daring thing you have ever done?
What is the hottest (i.e. spiciest) dish you have ever eaten?	What is the most physically demanding thing you have ever done?
What is the most worrying thing about the future?	What is the most impressive building or natural phenomena you have ever seen?
Which nationalities are (a) the friendliest (b) the least friendly?	What is the most surprising or shocking news item you have ever heard?

113 FILL IN THE MISSING WORDS

Fill in the missing words in the following text about Henry Ford I, the founder of Ford cars.

early	banned	because	against
easiest	could	or	by
immediately	demanded	in spite of	into
promptly	disliked	so	to
well	failed	that	until
	had learnt	when	up to
	had to	who	without
	rang		
	should		
	was sacked		
	wearing		
	were forbidden		
	were provided		

Fired for giving a present

Henry Ford I, the founder of mass car production, was not the (1)_____ of people to work for.

He (2)_____ chewing gum, so he (3)_____ it in his factories. Any worker (4)_____ disobeyed was sent to chew in the street for an hour (5)_____ pay.

Ford also (6)_____ complete silence and men (7)_____ to whistle, sing (8)_____ talk at their work.

One man who (9)_____ asked what he had done wrong. He was shown two photographs of himself taken (10)_____ a factory spy.

One showed him speaking to a colleague. In the other he was looking (11)_____ a doorway (12)_____ workers were not allowed to pass through.

Ford ruled that (13)_____ the starting bell (14)_____, men (15)_____ already be standing by their machines, (16)_____ their overalls.

They (17)_____ hang their street clothes on hooks that were (18)_____ whisked high out of reach.

To prevent anybody going home (19)_____, the hooks weren't lowered (20)_____ the end of the day.

No chairs (21)_____ but a worker found sitting on the floor or leaning against his machine was sacked. Employees who (22)_____ to wear their personal badges (23)_____ be sent home for (24)_____ a fortnight.

(25)_____ these rules, people clamoured for work (26)_____ jobs in the 1920s were hard to come by and Ford paid (27)_____.

A teenager was (28)_____ grateful at being hired that he bought his foreman a present.

He was (29)_____ dismissed because it was (30)_____ the rules to make a gift (31)_____ a superior.

That was his lesson. When he (32)_____ it, Ford gave him back his job.

114 FILL IN THE MISSING VERBS

Work in pairs. Fill in the missing verbs in the jokes below. Choose from the following. Use each verb once only. Make sure you choose the correct tense of the verb and also shortened forms (I've, we're, he's, etc.).

bite	fly	lay	sell	sting
bring	have	ring	sing	take
feel	invent	save	steal	use

Joke 1

I once knew a man who _____ a plot of land at the North Pole. He thought it was the ideal place to grow frozen peas.

Joke 2

A man _____ my uncle from drowning. He dragged him out of the sea, _____ him on the beach and said, 'I'll give you artificial respiration.'
My uncle said, 'No, give me the real thing. I'll pay for it.'

Joke 3

Teacher: Why aren't you writing, John?
John: I ain't got no pencil, sir.
Teacher: You ain't got no pencil? You haven't got a pencil, you mean.
John: Sir?
Teacher: I haven't got a pencil, he hasn't got a pencil, she hasn't got a pencil, we haven't got any pencils.
John: Blimey – who's _____ all the pencils?

Joke 4

1st dog owner: Tell me, has your dog got a family tree?
2nd dog owner: No, our dog doesn't mind which tree he _____.

Joke 5

'When I was on holiday at the seaside last year a crab _____ off one of my toes!'
'Which one?'
'I don't know. They all look alike to me.'

Joke 6

Singer: Do you like music?
Conductor: Yes. But please finish the song you _____.

Joke 7

Son: I _____ by a wasp!
Father: Don't worry. I'll put some special cream on it.
Son: That's no good. It _____ away now.

Joke 8

Janet: I _____ homesick.
George: But you are at home.
Janet: I know. But I'm sick of it.

Joke 9

'My uncle _____ a boomerang that wouldn't come back.'
'What did he call it?'
'A stick.'

Joke 10

The phone in the maternity ward of the hospital _____ and an excited voice said:
'I _____ in my wife. She's going to have a baby.'
'Is this her first baby?' asked the nurse.
'No, this is her husband!'

Joke 11

My mum had triplets once. The nurse came in with all three babies in her arms. She said to my dad, 'What do you think?'
He said, 'I _____ the middle one.'

Joke 12

'Doctor, these pills you gave me aren't doing me any good.'
'_____ you _____ two on an empty stomach, as I told you to?'
'Yes, doctor. But they kept rolling off!'

115 THIS IS THE NEWS

Work in groups. Imagine you are the producers of a 30-minute television news programme which is broadcast daily at 6 o'clock in the evening. If you had the following news items to choose from, which ones would you choose, in which order would you present each item and how long would each item last. (5 minutes maximum time per item.) You should also include one lighter item to close the programme with.

International news

1 Peace talks between Israel and Iraq have broken down.
2 500 people have been killed in a plane crash in Copenhagen.
3 The Mona Lisa has been stolen from the Louvre in Paris.
4 A new type of AIDS virus is spreading like wildfire throughout California.
5 The Japanese Prime Minister has been assassinated.
6 A fairly unknown Latvian poet has been awarded the Nobel Prize for Literature.
7 Nearly 2,000 people in Florida have been made homeless by the worst hurricane in that state for over 20 years.
8 Two top supermodels have been arrested in Bangkok and charged with drug-smuggling.
9 A flying saucer was seen by hundreds of people on the island of Crete.
10 The first brain transplant operation has been carried out on chimpanzees.
11 The computer company Apple has been taken over by IBM.
12 An explosion has been reported from a nuclear power station in the Ukraine.

Lighter item *(to finish off the program)*

1 A giant panda has been born at London zoo.
2 A woman who was rushed to hospital with severe stomach pains is still in a state of shock after having given birth to twins. (She didn't even know she was pregnant.)
3 A man missed his wedding in Manchester when he was put on the wrong train by his friends and ended up in Scotland.

Domestic/Home news

1 A man was shot down outside his home when he tried to stop a burglar.
2 The Prime Minister has been admitted to hospital after a minor heart attack.
3 Interest rates are to come down soon.
4 400 employees at the BBC have been made redundant.
5 TV celebrity has been caught shoplifting in Harrods.
6 The town of Chichester has been devastated by floods.
7 A member of the royal family has been linked romantically with a famous American pop star.
8 A small child has been abducted from a shopping centre in Coventry.

Sports news

1 England have been beaten by Iceland in their first qualifying match for the next World Cup.
2 The world record for the 1500 metres has been broken by an unknown Chinese athlete.
3 The next Winter Olympic Games is to be held in Sweden.
4 Manchester United have been drawn against Real Madrid in the semi-final of the European Cup.
5 An Italian football referee has been banned for life after it was found that he had accepted bribes to make sure that a certain team won.

When you have decided, write down your answers on a separate piece of paper. Then tell the class about your choice. Use the following phrases:

Firstly we'd have the story about...
Then we'd have...
After that / Next we'd have...
Finally, we'd have...

Index to structures used